How To
ANALYZE
FICTION

WILLIAM KENNEY

ASSISTANT PROFESSOR OF ENGLISH
MANHATTAN COLLEGE

**MONARCH
PRESS**

Published by
MONARCH PRESS
a Simon & Schuster division of
Gulf & Western Corporation
Simon & Schuster Building
1230 Avenue of the Americas
New York, N.Y. 10020

MONARCH PRESS and colophon are trademarks of Simon
& Schuster, registered in the U.S. Patent and Trademark
Office.

Standard Book Number: 0-671-18746-5

Printed in the United States of America

CONTENTS

PREFACE

The title of this book is *How to Analyze Fiction*. I presume that the word "analyze" will immediately evoke hostile responses in many of my readers. "Why must we always *analyze* everything?" thousands of students have asked hundreds of teachers. "Why can't we just enjoy what we read?"

It's a fair question. Enjoyment is, quite properly, what most of us seek in our reading of fiction. And, for all the occasional sneers directed at "mere entertainment," it would be very hard indeed to make a convincing case for the superiority of unentertaining fiction.

We may agree, then, that enjoyment, and not analysis, is our end. We want to enjoy what we read. In fact, we want to get the fullest possible measure of enjoyment out of every story that we read. At least, it is on this assumption that this book is written.

This brings us back to the subject of analysis. For it is my position that analysis, properly understood and rightly undertaken, contributes essentially to the full enjoyment of fiction.

Properly understood. For what do we mean by analysis? According to many students, to analyze is "to tear things to pieces." Well, that sounds unpleasant enough. In fact, it's a rather violent way to describe what goes on in most classrooms. But analysis is not quite tearing things to pieces. Or, at least, it's a good deal more than that.

To analyze a literary work is to identify the separate parts that make it up (this corresponds roughly to the notion of tearing it to pieces), to determine the relationships among the parts, and to discover the relation of the parts to the whole. If some analyses do seem to leave the work torn to pieces, figuratively speaking, this means simply that they are not complete analyses. The end of the analysis is always the understanding of the literary work as a unified and complex whole.

And analysis must be not only properly understood but also rightly undertaken. Analysis itself can often be drudgery, whether the analysis be of a literary work, a chemical compound, or a competitive sport. And the analysis of a literary work has still more to be said against it: it is bound to be artificial. The "parts" we discern in our analyses exist, after all, rather in the mind of the reader than in the works themselves. To illustrate this point, let's consider a sentence we might find in a work of fiction: "The windows of the old house rattled as John slammed the door." To what "part" of the story might such a sentence belong?

Well, since the sentence tells of an event, we might be inclined to think of it as a matter of plot. But surely to be told that John is the kind of person who slams doors is to learn something about John. Not plot, then, but character. Look again. The door slammed by John is in an old house with windows that rattle. Setting? Which is it? The answer, of course, is all three. And, in the context of a complete story, this same sentence may have several further functions in addition to those already suggested. The house, for instance, might have some sort of symbolic value. And of course the sentence might be examined as an example of the author's style.

Analysis, then, may be drudgery and is certainly artificial. Why should we indulge in it at all?

Any athlete knows that practice in any sport is drudgery. And he knows, too, that practice is often artificial. Tackling a dummy is not the same as tackling an opponent—certainly not the same as tackling an opponent who is trying to disappear behind a massive wall of blockers in a championship game with the score 7-7 in the closing minutes of the last quarter. But he knows that the purpose of the practice session is to develop his skills, his co-ordination, and his reflexes so that he can make the tackle without stopping to think about it—that is, without analyzing what he's doing.

Literary analysis of the sort this book invites you to undertake may be compared to practice in a sport. By analysis, you will develop intellectual and emotional skills, co-ordination, and reflexes to the point where you'll be able to use them without stopping to think of what you're doing. You'll become aware of many of the things that go on in fiction, in the hope that eventually this awareness will operate as you read, rather than in a classroom post-mortem. What the inexperienced reader discovers by painful analysis, the experienced reader grasps, so it seems, by instinct. But in most cases the "instinct" has been developed by experience in analysis.

Analysis rightly undertaken, then, is analysis undertaken for the ultimate purpose of making analysis unnecessary. Your goal should be to develop, by the exercise of analysis, your skills as a reader so that eventually you may move on from the work of analyzing fiction to the joy of experiencing it.

The present book makes no claims to originality, either in content or format. I have felt that what the reader wants is the clearest possible concise exposition of established notions of fiction, rather than original but possibly erratic theories.

CHAPTER 1

PLOT

CHOICE

FICTION AND CHOICE: The act of writing, whether one is writing a complex three-volume novel or a personal letter to a close friend, consists of a series of choices. To see just what this means, let's consider the simpler form, the personal letter, first.

CHOICE IN A PERSONAL LETTER: In writing a personal letter, we begin making choices at the very beginning—at the salutation as it is usually called. We begin "Dear————." Dear what? Analyzing our relationship to the intended recipient of the letter permits us to choose the saluation properly. If the letter is to a personal friend, we choose to address him by his first name, perhaps even by a nickname. A more distant acquaintance calls for a more formal salutation, a more intimate one may suggest a more intimate salutation. On the one hand, "Dear Mr. Brown," on the other, "Darling." The choice is ours.

Of course, the choice is not entirely free. We are limited to some extent by custom, to some extent by what we understand as the expectations of the person who is to read the letter. Still, we must decide what custom applies to the particular situation in which we find ourselves. We must decide to what extent we are going to be bound by custom. And we must decide just what are the expectations of the person to whom we address ourselves. And we may have to decide whether there is some good reason to disappoint those expectations. For instance, she may expect me to address her as "Darling," since I normally do, but I want her to know at once that I'm displeased with her: "Dear Mary."

Many of the choices we make in these situations are, of course, not conscious choices. Most often, we instinctively choose the right salutation and make similarly correct choices right down to the closing ("Sincerely"? "Love"?). But conscious or not, all of them are significant. All of them contribute to the total meaning we communicate to the reader.

CHOICE IN WRITING A STORY: The writer of fiction, like the writer of a letter, faces a series of choices. Some of the choices he makes are fully conscious; some are not. But all are significant; all contribute to making the story what it is and not another thing.

Further, the writer of fiction must recognize that there are limits to the choices available to him. Conventions, in some cases established by the practice of writers over many centuries, have led to the development of expectations on the part of readers. The writer must take these conventions and expectations into account. But he must decide for himself what conventions are appropriate to what he is doing. He must decide to what extent he is willing to follow convention. He must decide which of the reader's expectations are relevant to the sort of story he is writing. And he may decide that he is justified in violating the reader's expectations for the sake of some higher purpose.

CHOICE AND THE READER: What have the choices facing the writer to do with the experience of the reader of fiction? I suggest that the best way to develop a full awareness of what's going on in any story you may read is to develop an awareness of the choices the author has made, the choices that have given the story its distinctive shape. This includes, of course, an awareness of the alternatives open to the author. Your purpose is not to determine why the author made these choices (often he's not sure himself), but rather to discover how the author's choices have combined to produce the unified story you have before you.

THE CHOICE OF SUBJECT: It is natural to think of the author's series of choices as beginning with the choice of subject. In fact, however, the writer may not begin by thinking in terms of subject at all. A chance remark, a fleeting insight into character, a striking image—any of these may be the true origin of a story. Such matters are, however, more relevant to the author's biography or to a study of the creative process than to the analysis of a particular story. If the writer does not always begin with a subject, the reader is inclined to begin by wondering what the story is about—which is one way of saying what the subject is. And this is surely a question (again, perhaps not consciously asked) that the writer must answer early in the process of writing his story.

But of course the writer, unlike the reader, does not merely discover his subject; he chooses it, although the choice may be so instinctively made as to seem almost a discovery.

SUBJECT

THE MEANING OF SUBJECT: Words like "subject," "content," "form," and "style" are so freely used in discussions of literature that we must always be sure of what we mean by them. Often "subject" and "content" are treated as synonyms. In this book, they are not. "Content" as I use the word means what the work contains. Content is essentially identical with form. We may sometimes find it desirable, for purposes of discussion, to act as though there were a distinction between the two, but we should do this as seldom as possible (for it's a bad habit to get into) and we should always remain aware that the distinction is even more artificial than most literary distinctions.

Subject, on the other hand, is not what the work contains but what the work refers to. Unlike the content, the subject exists before the story is written and would exist if the story were never written. For instance, we might consider the problems of a certain kind of middle-class woman as the subject of Gustave Flaubert's famous novel *Madame Bovary* (I don't suggest this is the only possible formulation of that novel's subject), while the content of the novel is something infinitely more complex.

THE SIGNIFICANCE OF SUBJECT: It should be clear from

what has been said that no subject, as we are using the term, is good or bad in itself. The problems of middle-class women existed before Flaubert chose them as his subject. These problems could provide subjects for an infinite number of novels, some good, some bad, some mediocre. If *Madame Bovary* is a superior novel, then, it is not because of its subject.

SUBJECT AND THE READER: Yet it is undeniable that some readers, while perhaps agreeing that you can't tell a book by its cover, do tend to select books by their subjects. One reader, and probably a very nice lady at that, likes to read stories about young love but won't read anything on the subject of war, while another reader's tastes may be exactly the reverse of this. I once recommended a movie to a friend, one of the most intelligent men I know, and he replied he didn't think he'd see it because he didn't like movies about doctors. I pointed out to my friend, an ardent admirer of Herman Melville's *Moby Dick,* that this was rather like saying that one doesn't like novels about white whales, but he remained unconvinced.

This kind of prejudice is unfortunate. The reader who succumbs to it is needlessly cutting himself off from many of the pleasures that good literature (and good movies) can give. It is wisest to grant the writer his choice of subject and look to see how subject is transformed into content. That is, judge the story, not the subject.

SUBJECT AND THE WRITER: But if no subject is good or bad in itself, a subject may be good or bad for a particular writer. We may assume that every writer will find there are some subjects he simply cannot transform into content, some subjects he is incapable of turning into stories. He will find, on the other hand, that some subjects are particularly suited to his talents and temperament. Indeed, some writers (D. H. Lawrence, for one) seem to find a particularly congenial subject early in their careers and return to it again and again as they mature. Some writers, even some very good ones, may be felt to have only one real subject in the entire body of their work.

Whether a writer has one subject or many, he must choose

those subjects to which he is capable of giving the fullest artistic response—and, as regards his subject, this is all we may legitimately ask.

THE EXAMPLE OF JANE AUSTEN: The English novelist Jane Austen (1775-1817), author of such famous works as *Pride and Prejudice* and *Emma,* is an excellent example of a writer wise in choice of subject. Miss Austen lived in one of the most eventful periods of British history, but her own life was rather uneventful. As a novelist, she drew not on the Napoleonic wars, about which she was probably not very well informed and of which she of course had no firsthand knowledge, but on the quiet provincial life with which she was entirely familiar. To those for whom "subjects" have some sort of intrinsic value, Miss Austen's choice may seem foolish. Yet in choosing, not the big subject with little personal meaning for her, but the little subject to which her complex, ironic personality fully responded, Jane Austen was making the only choice a genuine novelist could make. And the proof that her choice was wise is the greatness of the novels that choice led to. Today, Jane Austen is universally recognized as one of the greatest (some would say *the* greatest) of English novelists.

FROM SUBJECT TO STORY: To judge a work of fiction by its subject, then, is as ill-advised as to judge a book by its cover. The question is how the author transforms his subject into content, that is, how he makes a story out of a subject.

THE READER'S EXPECTATIONS: At this point it might be advisable to remind ourselves of what we commonly expect of a work of fiction. In specific details, the nature of these expectations will differ from reader to reader. Yet we will surely find one element common to every reader's expectations before a work of fiction. That is, the expectation that the work will tell a story.

WHAT IS A STORY?:   But what precisely do we mean when we say that fiction tells a story? At the minimum, we mean that a work of fiction deals with events that occur in temporal sequence—that is, one after another. The story of a man's life, for example, will include his birth, his growing up, his marriage, his growing old, his death. Obviously, these events occur over a period of time. More commonly, of course, a story will deal with a more limited series of events. A young man meets a girl, he is attracted to her, he courts her, he proposes marriage, she accepts, they quarrel, they separate, they patch up their differences, they marry. The temporal element is still clear.

Yet any experienced reader of fiction knows there is more to it than this. A story deals with events that occur in temporal sequence, to be sure, but a slavish adherence to temporal sequence is rare in serious fiction. Consider, for example, F. Scott Fitzgerald's novel *The Great Gatsby*. In this famous work, we are told of Gatsby as a boy planning to "study needed inventions" and of the mature Gatsby shot to death in his swimming pool. Now Gatsby was obviously a small boy before he was a man. Yet Fitzgerald does not tell us directly of Gatsby the boy until after Gatsby's death. The novel departs, in this and in other instances, from strict temporal sequence.

We may say in fact that every story involves some sort of departure from strict temporal sequence. At the very least, we must be prepared for gaps in the sequence. Structurally, Ernest Hemingway's "The Killers" is an unusually straightforward story. There is none of the kind of juggling with time we have noted in *The Great Gatsby*. Yet even Hemingway, while keeping his story moving forward in time, selects some moments for inclusion while rejecting others. What is presented happens in temporal sequence, but not everything is presented. There are gaps.

PLOT

THE NATURE OF PLOT: What this seems to imply is that the simple setting down of events in temporal sequence is not the main concern of the writer of fiction. Other things are more important to him. It is in arranging the events of his story according to demands other than the purely temporal that the author creates plot.

In other words, plot reveals events to us, not only in their temporal, but also in their causal relationships. Plot makes us aware of events not merely as elements in a temporal series but also as an intricate pattern of cause and effect. Nick's decision, at the end of "The Killers," to leave the town in which the story is set is one event in a series. But it is also the effect of the events that have preceded it, the implications of those events, and the impact of events and implications on Nick. Gatsby's death and dismal funeral in Fitzgerald's novel must be seen as the final effects of a causal chain that can be traced all the way back to his boyhood. And, as Fitzgerald's novel indicates, the writer of fiction is willing to manipulate temporal relationships boldly for the sake of revealing with the greatest amount of force the causal relationships that are his principal concern.

By plot in fiction, then, we mean not simply the events recounted in the story but the author's arrangement of those events according to their causal relationships.

THE STRUCTURE OF PLOT: To recognize this much, however, is only a beginning. We must consider in more specific terms the form this "arrangement" we call plot is likely to take. For, underlying the evident diversity of fiction, we may discern certain recurring patterns.

We may seem to be belaboring the obvious if we note that one discernible pattern is the division of the story into beginning, middle, and end. But if we remind ourselves that a story is a series of choices, this apparently crude division may come to seem more significant. The writer chooses to begin his story at one point and end it at another. And, as we have seen, he need not feel bound by temporal sequence in moving from beginning through middle to end. The pattern of beginning-middle-end is therefore a pattern of choices—that is, a meaningful pattern.

BEGINNING: We expect a story to begin at the beginning. Now in a story like "The Killers" the beginning may be what comes first in time, but *The Great Gatsby* illustrates that this is not always so. What we want to know, then, is what, besides temporal sequence, determines the choice of a beginning.

Rather than losing ourselves in abstractions at this point, let's examine the beginning—specifically, the first paragraph—of a very famous story, Nathaniel Hawthorne's "Young Goodman Brown."

> Young Goodman Brown came forth at sunset into the street at Salem village; but put his head back, after crossing the threshold, to exchange a parting kiss with his young wife. And Faith, as the wife was aptly named, thrust her own pretty head into the street, letting the wind play with the pink ribbons of her cap while she called to Goodman Brown.

EXPOSITION: The first thing we may note about this paragraph is that it provides us with a certain amount of information. We are introduced to the story's title character; we are informed that he has a wife; we are told her name; we are told that, like her husband, she is young; and we are told that she is pretty. We are also informed that Brown and his wife live in Salem village. Now Salem, we know, is a city in Massachusetts. The word "village," however, indicates the historical setting of the story: it takes place before Salem became a city. Finally, we are informed that Young Goodman Brown is parting from his wife. We are not told at this point whether he is going on a trivial errand or a long journey. This information is given a bit later in the story; the beginning is not here, nor is it usually, limited to a single paragraph.

The name usually given to the process by which the writer imparts to the reader information necessary to the understanding of the story is "exposition," and exposition is normally a primary function of the beginning of any story.

THE ELEMENT OF INSTABILITY: It is seldom, in fiction of any merit, that the beginning, however expository it may seem, does not imply more than the facts it presents. For the situation with which the story begins must have a certain openness, must be capable of some sort of development, or else there would be no story. In short, we may expect that the situation with which the story begins will contain within it a hidden or overt element of instability.

What evidence of instability, whether hidden or overt, do we find in the first paragraph of "Young Goodman Brown"? Apparently, Hawthorne is presenting a picture of an almost ideally happy marriage. We note, for instance, that the young husband, even after starting out, pauses to kiss his wife. Yet, there are unsettling elements in this paragraph.

First of all, the young couple are parting. Again, we do not know at this point for how long they will be apart. Yet we know that any separation is a potential challenge to the stability of a relationship. Secondly, there are certain ambiguities in the presentation of the young wife. She is, we are told, aptly named Faith. Still, the image of the wind playing with the ribbons of her cap is disturbing. For one thing, the detail of the pink ribbons, combined with her prettiness, makes us suspect the possibility of vanity as a quality of Faith's character, and vanity is always a potential source of instability. Finally, the story is set in Salem village. Any reasonably informed reader must be aware of the Salem witch hunts of the seventeenth century. Naturally, we wonder if witchcraft is to play a part in the story about to unfold.

In short, while the first paragraph of Hawthorne's story seems on a superficial first reading an almost idyllic picture of marital bliss, certain troubling details will make the sensitive reader aware of the potential instability in the situation. This awareness will, of course, become more precise as the story progresses. Eventually, the reader will see which of the potential sources of instability constitute the real threat to the apparent stability of the individual situation and what form this threat will take. As these points become clear, we move from the beginning to the middle of the story.

The beginning of a story then, in addition to the necessary exposition, gives us the picture of a situation in which there exist sources of instability, which may at the outset be latent or overt. In these respects, the beginning of "Young Goodman Brown" is typical. But it should not be concluded that the beginning of every story will be in all details like that of this story. Again, the author has a number of choices open to him.

CHOICE AND BEGINNINGS: The beginning of "Young Goodman Brown" is scenic, a term whose meaning will be made
clear in Chapter 5. For the moment, let us just observe that
Hawthorne begins his story with the direct presentation of
two characters in action, rather than with a more generalized
sort of introductory passage. The beginning of "My Kinsman,
Major Molineux," another story by Hawthorne, is quite different:

> After the kings of Great Britain had assumed the right
> of appointing the colonial governors, the measures of the
> latter seldom met with the ready and generous approba-
> tion which had been paid to those of their predecessors,
> under the original charters. The people looked with most
> jealous scrutiny to the exercise of power which did not
> emanate from themselves, and they usually rewarded
> their rulers with slender gratitude for the compliances by
> which, in softening their instructions from beyond the
> sea, they had incurred the reprehension of those who
> gave them. . . .

The story is, then, placed explicitly in a historical setting, which
is presented to us in general terms before the introduction of
any specific action or characters. Why Hawthorne chose one
kind of beginning for "Young Goodman Brown" and another
for "My Kinsman, Major Molineux" is not a question we need
settle here. Both beginnings, we should note, fulfill an expository function, while suggesting (more explicitly in "My Kinsman, Major Molineux") sources of instability in the initial
situation.

THE MIDDLE—CONFLICT, COMPLICATION, CLIMAX: We move
from the end of the beginning to the beginning of the middle
as the elements tending towards instability in the initial situation group themselves into what we recognize as a pattern of
conflict. In "Young Goodman Brown" this pattern emerges
upon Brown's encounter with a strange man in the forest.
Brown has been thinking of what is to happen that night and
musing that knowledge of it would kill his wife, Faith. The
strange man has been expecting Brown and is, it seems, to be
his companion for the evening. But Brown indicates that he

wishes to return home. It is in Brown's attempt to resist the will of his companion that the conflict becomes evident.

Note that this conflict is related to the elements of instability we observed in the very first paragraph of the story. To be sure, the suggestion of weakness in Faith's character is not yet developed. But the possible dangers in a parting from loved ones are certainly involved in Young Goodman Brown's journey into a dark forest where terrible work is to be done. And the diabolical overtones of this must remind us of the hints of witchcraft we find in the Salem setting.

COMPLICATION AND CLIMAX: Just as a development towards conflict is latent in the initial situation, so is a development toward climax latent in the initial conflict. The movement from the initial statement of conflict to the climax is often referred to as complication. The climax is reached when the complication attains its highest point of intensity, from which point the outcome of the story is inevitable.

In "Young Goodman Brown," the complication consists primarily of the diabolical rites to which the stranger (who is, we are told, the Devil) leads the half-resisting Brown. Also included is the process by which the hero's resistance is weakened until he numbers himself among the converts to the diabolical religion whose rites are being celebrated. But the hero's conversion is not itself the climax. This, the story's highest point of intensity, occurs when Brown finds that his wife, Faith, the wife he had believed would be killed by the very thought of such evil practices, is among the converts.

The importance of complication in fiction cannot be overestimated. Without adequate complication, the conflict would remain inert, its possibilities never realized. And it is by his control of complication that the writer gradually increases the intensity of his narrative, thus preparing us to receive the full impact of the climax. As a rough measure of the importance of complication, examination will reveal that the largest part of "Young Goodman Brown," as of any great work of fiction, is devoted to complication. It is hardly an overstatement to say that it is in his invention and control of complication that the great writer of fiction most fully reveals his genius.

THE END: In our three-part division of the work of fiction, the end consists of everything from the climax to the *denouement,* or outcome of the story. In "Young Goodman Brown" the end is devoted to the aftermath of Brown's experience in the forest. Shattered by what has happened, he lives out his life in misery, and, we are told, "his dying hour was gloom."

We began by discussing the structure of plot in terms of beginning, middle, and end. We may now see that the beginning takes us from exposition to the initial statement of conflict; the middle, from conflict through complication to climax; and the end, from climax to denouement.

A NOTE ON CONFLICT: The conflicts with which fiction concerns itself are of many kinds. A story may deal with a conflict within a single man (e.g., desire vs. duty), a conflict between men, a conflict between man and society, between man and nature, and so on. You may often find it helpful to state the conflict of a story in terms applicable to a sports event or court case, for example, A vs. B, the hero's individual conscience vs. the demands of society. How would you state the conflict of a story in terms applicable to a sport?

THE LAWS OF PLOT

In forming the particular plot of his story, the writer may be expected to follow certain laws. When we speak of the laws of plot, we do not mean the kinds of laws passed by legislative bodies. We mean rather generalizations drawn from the practice of the best writers through the ages. To deviate from these laws is not, therefore, a crime. Still, we may expect that writers of the future will continue to follow the basic principles observed by their great predecessors. In fact, apparent deviations from these laws will often turn out on closer inspection to be not deviations at all, but new applications of the old principles.

PLAUSIBILITY: Of the laws governing plot in fiction, one of the most important is certainly the law of plausibility. To say that a story has plausibility is simply to say that it is convincing on its own terms.

There are, then, two steps involved in judging whether a story has plausibility. For before we can determine whether a story is convincing on its own terms, we must recognize what those terms are.

The demand for plausibility must not, for instance, be confused with the demand for realism. We have a right to demand that a story be plausible; at least, the great works of fiction always have been plausible. We have no right to demand that a story be realistic, for realism is only one of the many modes of fiction.

A story is plausible when it is true to itself. Skeptical readers may find it unrealistic that the Devil appears as a character in "Young Goodman Brown." But even these readers must admit that, if we accept the Devil's direct intrusion in human affairs as a premise, the rest of the story is perfectly convincing.

Consider the denouement, for instance. Brown's "dying hour was gloom." Note how naturally this flows from what has gone before. Brown dies in gloom because he is unable to bear the insight into man's sinful nature he has received in the forest. And this insight is unbearable because, before going into the forest, Brown had an idealized, rather than realistic, view of human nature. This idealized view had made him believe that his wife, Faith, would be killed by the very thought of sin. He was unable to see her as human, that is, as capable of sin—just as he is capable of sin. And his extreme reaction to his new insight is entirely plausible, for just as Faith seemed totally good to him before, now she seems totally evil. At the end of the story, as at the beginning, Brown is unable to accept the truth that human nature is mixed. There is, then, a consistency underlying the superficial reversal in Brown's character and outlook. And this consistency is the basis of the story's plausibility, of its truth to itself.

SURPRISE: Plausibility, we have said, implies a story's truth to itself. Now this seems to suggest that a story's end is somehow contained in its beginning. In a sense, this is true. At the same time, a story that never surprises us is likely to prove rather dull reading. But how may the apparently contradictory claims of surprise and plausibility be reconciled?

An answer may be suggested by the simple example of the pure detective story. When, at the end of the second-to-last chapter in a novel by John Dickson Carr or Agatha Christie, the murderer's identity is revealed, we want to be surprised. Indeed, if we are not surprised we quite rightly consider this a flaw in the novel.

But then we turn to the last chapter. For a detective novel does not usually end with the identification of the murderer. After he has identified the murderer, the great detective proceeds to explain the process of reasoning by which he has arrived at his solution. And now we want to be convinced that the solution which seemed so surprising was in fact inevitable—the only possible solution in the light of the evidence. And again, if this demand is not satisfied, we feel that the novel is flawed.

Now what is explicit, even mechanical, in the detective story is implicit in all good fiction. We want to be surprised, but then we want to be satisfied that the surprise does not violate the basic law of plausibility. Is it surprising that Faith is at the dark rites of the forest? It is also plausible. We are, after all, all sinners. And we are not asked to accept Faith's presence until it has been made clear that virtually the entire population of Salem village, including the preacher and Brown's own parents, is also present. Finally, we recall that, at the very beginning of the story, we saw in the pink ribbons in Faith's hair the pathetic flag of her human frailty.

SUSPENSE: A third law governing plot is that a good plot arouses suspense. By suspense we mean an expectant uncertainty as to the outcome of the story. True suspense is more than a matter of not knowing how things will turn out. I don't know how things turn out in hundreds of stories that I've never read, but I'm hardly in suspense about them. The suspense of which we speak involves some awareness of the possibilities and, ideally, some concern about them. Suspense develops as we become aware of the incipient instability in a situation. In "Young Goodman Brown," for instance, we are in suspense as soon as we are aware that Faith might be in the forest. Our suspense as to this point is relieved when we learn that she is there.

A device conducive to suspense is *foreshadowing*. By this we mean introducing details which hint at the direction the story is going to take. Hawthorne, for instance, introduces details that suggest Faith's presence before explicitly revealing her presence to us. He thus builds up in us the expectation (not, however, the certainty) that she will be there, then satisfies that expectation.

PLOT AND UNITY: The one overriding demand we commonly make of plot is that it have unity. It should be clear by now that a plot that fits the description suggested in the present chapter must inevitably have unity. Any plot that has a true beginning, middle, and end and that follows the laws of plausibility, surprise, and suspense must have unity, for that is all we mean by unity.

SUBPLOTS: A special problem relating to unity arises in some longer works of fiction. This is the problem of the subplot, by which is meant a sequence of events distinct, at least in part, from the main plot. Where a subplot exists, we may expect that one of two things is true. First, the subplot may be closely related to the main plot, for instance as an analogy to the main plot. The clearest example of this comes not from fiction but from drama. In Shakespeare's *King Lear* the subplot involving Gloucester and his sons is clearly analogous to the main plot involving Lear and his daughters. A second possibility is that the work's principle of unity is to be found in some element other than plot—for instance in theme, which will be discussed in Chapter 7.

If neither of these two conditions is met, the subplot compromises the unity of the work as a whole and is to that extent a flaw. A work flawed in this way may still be excellent, however. The episode of "The Man on the Hill" in Henry Fielding's *Tom Jones* is generally considered a violation of unity, but few would deny that *Tom Jones* is one of the great English novels. The explanation of this judgment is that, apart from this one flaw, *Tom Jones* has one of the most intricately unified plots in the history of the novel and also has virtues other than unity (e.g., vitality) which must be taken into account in any adequate evaluation.

PLOT AS UNITY: As this discussion suggests, plot may be the single most important device making for unity in a particular story. In organizing events into beginning, middle, and end, the author is imposing on, or discovering in, the raw material of experience that sense of order which is what we mean by unity in art.

PLOT AS EXPRESSION: It would be unfortunate if this analytic discussion of plot seemed to suggest that plotting is merely a mechanical process. In fact, plot is of the highest importance in expressing the meaning of a work of fiction. It is through plot that the author organizes the raw material of experience, and an author's way of organizing experience must tell us a great deal about his way of understanding experience—that is, about the meaning experience has for him. Surely our sense of the meaning of experience is closely tied to our understanding of what causes what, and it is the business of plot to clarify causal relationships. To recognize the cause of Goodman Brown's gloom is to recognize the meaning of his story.

We may conclude, then, that an understanding of plot is the most important factor in the understanding of fiction. Plot, says Aristotle, is the soul of tragedy. It may well be the soul of fiction, too.

CHAPTER 2

CHARACTER

INTRODUCTION: In the preceding chapter we saw that plot results from a series of choices made by the author. Another way of saying the same thing is that plot is artificial. There are no plots in life; plot is the imposition of form on experience that is essentially formless.

Now, even the reader who has never before thought of the question in these terms should have little difficulty accepting this view of plot. We are all really aware, however vaguely, that plot is artificial, that it is something made up.

The reader may find it more difficult, however, to think of character in these terms. For, if there are no plots in life, there certainly are people. And most of us tend to expect the people —or "characters"—in fiction to be similar to the people in life. To say of a fictional character that he is "artificial" is usually to imply disapproval. Whatever degree of artifice we are willing to allow in plot, we expect characters to be "natural" or "lifelike."

LIFELIKENESS

THE STANDARD OF LIFELIKENESS: It is the argument of this chapter that the standard of lifelikeness is inadequate for judging character in fiction. At best, the notion of lifelikeness is an oversimplification. A fictional character must be other things besides lifelike, and the standard of lifelikeness doesn't help us to understand very much about the ways in which character is presented in fiction.

But apart from being an oversimplification, the standard of lifelikeness may be downright misleading, especially if taken too literally. That is, the search for lifelikeness may lead the reader to overlook much that is essential in literary characterization.

Just what do we mean when we say a character should be lifelike? What kind of life should a character be like? If we insist that characters should be like the people we know, aren't we imposing an excessively severe limitation on the author's creative powers? Would the great characters of fiction meet this test? Would Hamlet? Don Quixote? Captain Ahab?

I am not suggesting that we should entirely ignore the relation between fictional characters and real human beings. Rather, I am saying we should recognize that this relation is a complex, not a simple one. We should be aware, then, not only of the similarities but also of the differences between fictional characters and real human beings.

CHARACTER AND FREEDOM: Whatever is true of the amount of freedom human beings enjoy, the fictional character is never entirely free. For, unlike the real human being, the fictional character is part of an artistic whole and must always serve the needs of that whole. One of the most delicate tasks of the writer of fiction is to create and maintain the illusion that his characters are free, while at the same time making sure they are not really so. For a really free character would be free of his duty to the story of which he is a part. And a story which admitted such freedom could never achieve unity. The necessity of being fitted into a satisfying artistic whole is the most important difference between the fictional character and the human being and is the basis of all the other differences.

CHARACTER AND CHOICE: It is not enough, then, for a writer to be able to observe human nature and, from his observations, to imagine lifelike characters. The necessity of placing character in a unified work of art forces the author into a series of choices. He must always be prepared to sacrifice one interest—for instance, the interest of "lifelikeness" in character for its own sake—for the sake of others, for instance, the interest in plot, in theme, in the unity of the whole. At the same time, he must make sure that the choices he is forced to make do not become too obvious, for he wants us to concentrate on the story, not on the difficulties he had in writing it.

THE STANDARD OF RELEVANCE: Any discussion of character
in fiction, then, must attend to the relationships between character and the other elements of the story, and between character and the story as a whole. That is, character must be
considered as part of the story's internal structure.

But just as we ultimately refer the story as a whole to the
real world in which we live our lives, so we may refer character
to the real human beings who inhabit that world. Essentially,
we refer the fictional characters to ourselves. I am the human
being I know best.

At this point the standard of lifelikeness may seem to suggest
itself once again. But the limitations of that standard should
now be even more clear. For if we ask that the characters be
like ourselves or like the people we know, we are not only
setting boundaries on the writer's imagination, but we may also
be overlooking the function of character within the story.

More to the point than the standard of lifelikeness is the standard of relevance. According to this standard, the question is not
whether the fictional character is like me. Rather, the question
is, what has he to do with me. In other words, what is the
character's relevance to me.

UNIVERSAL AND PARTICULAR: The advantage of the standard of relevance is that it allows the author a full measure of
freedom in the creation of character without denying the point
of contact between the character and the reader. Theoretically,
the author can range from the pure type, representing one universal quality, to the most eccentric of individuals. He is bound
only by the reader's demand that the characters in fiction be in
some way relevant to his own experience.

It should be noted that a character may be far removed from
the "average" or "normal" without becoming irrelevant to the
reader. In William Faulkner's novel *The Sound and the Fury,*
Benjy, one of the principal characters, is literally an idiot. An
important part of the novel is told from Benjy's point of view

(point of view is discussed in Chapter 4). The standard of life-likeness would be of little help in judging Faulkner's success in portraying Benjy. How can a reader who is not himself an idiot determine whether Faulkner faithfully presents the workings of an idiot's mind? If Faulkner's portrayal of Benjy is generally admired, it is because most readers feel the relevance of Benjy.

FORMS OF RELEVANCE: What do we mean when we say that a character as different from the average reader as Benjy is is still relevant to the reader? There are essentially two ways in which a character can be relevant.

A character is obviously relevant to us and to our experience if he is like ourselves or like others whom we know. Lifelikeness, then, is properly understood as one form of relevance. A character is relevant if there are a lot of people like him in the real world.

But, as we have already noted, the world does not contain many Hamlets, Don Quixotes, or Captain Ahabs. Are these characters, so often numbered among the great literary creations, therefore irrelevant to us? If so, then either the standard of relevance is worthless, or the critical judgment of generations has been mistaken.

What we must do is to recognize a second form of relevance. There are not many Don Quixotes around, but there is something of Don Quixote in each of us. It is in this sense that we feel his relevance to us. And it may be that this form of relevance, rather than lifelikeness, is the secret of the power the great characters of fiction hold for us.

JUDGING FICTIONAL CHARACTERS: In judging fictional characters, then, there are certain questions that seem appropriate. Two of the most important are: What is the relevance of this character to me? In what ways does he contribute to the story of which he is part? Any judgment that ignores either of these questions will probably be inadequate.

SIMPLE AND COMPLEX CHARACTERS

The preceding paragraph suggests standards for judging fictional characters. But before these or any standards may be responsibly applied it is necessary to examine more clearly the portrayal of character in fiction. We have to know more about the kinds of characters that appear in fiction and about the means by which character is portrayed.

With regard to the kinds of characters portrayed, it may be helpful to follow the practice of many critics and divide fictional characters into two general categories. Our names for these categories will be simple characters and complex characters. Other critics, in making essentially the same division, sometimes use different terms. One of the most suggestive statements of the distinction we have in mind is that of E. M. Forster, who, in his *Aspects of the Novel,* divides the characters of fiction into "flat" and "round" characters.

SIMPLE (FLAT) CHARACTERS: The simple, or flat, character is less the representation of a human personality than the embodiment of a single attitude or obsession in a character. Forster calls this kind of character flat because we see only one side of him.

Included among simple characters are all the familiar types, or stereotypes, of fiction. The mark of the stereotyped character is that he can be summed up adequately in a formula: the noble savage, the trusted old family retainer, and the poor but honest working girl are a few familiar fictional types.

Not all simple characters, however, are stereotypes like those referred to above. The essence of the sterotype may be expressed in a formula that applies to a large number of fictional characters, drawn from a large number of works of fiction. We must recognize the existence of a second kind of simple character. Like the stereotype, this kind of character may be summed up in a formula. But he differs from the stereotype in that his formula is his own; there is no other character in fiction whom it exactly fits.

An Example from Dickens: The works of Charles Dickens are filled with examples of this second kind of simple character. Consider, for instance, Uriah Heep in Dickens' novel *David Copperfield*. Uriah is certainly a simple character; his personality is made up of very few elements. In fact, he may be described as no more than an embodiment of his peculiar kind of "humility." The point is that his humility is of a peculiar kind. Uriah Heep is a simple character but he is not a stereotype, because there is no one else quite like him in fiction.

COMPLEX (ROUND) CHARACTERS: At the other end of the spectrum is the complex character, called round by Forster because we see all sides of him. The complex character is obviously more lifelike than the simple, because in life people are not simply embodiments of single attitudes. It would be pointless to list examples of complex characters from fiction. If Dickens is a master of the simple character, most of the great English novelists excel in portraying complex characters. Becky Sharp, the protagonist of Thackeray's *Vanity Fair,* is one example; the husband, Rawdon Crawley, is another. In fact, *Vanity Fair* abounds in brilliantly portrayed complex characters.

If the mark of the simple character is that he can be summed up adequately in a formula, the mark of the complex character is that he is capable of surprising us. Rawdon Crawley's deepening sense of responsibility in *Vanity Fair,* for instance, is surprising in the light of the first impression he makes. But in character, as in plot, surprise must not arise from a violation of plausibility. Thackeray's portrayal of Rawdon Crawley is one of the great examples in English fiction of a writer's convincing us of profound changes in one of his characters. And his success is based in large part on our awareness, which may become conscious awareness only in the process of analysis, that the seeds of change, and of precisely this kind of change, have been present in Rawdon from the start.

GRADATIONS IN COMPLEXITY: In contrasting simple and complex characters above, I used the metaphor of the spectrum. This was not accidental. For characters in fiction should not be thought of as existing in sealed compartments, one marked "simple," the other "complex." The metaphor of the spectrum, connoting subtle differences in gradation as we move from the simple to the complex, is more to the point. Captain Ahab, in Melville's *Moby Dick,* is certainly closer to the simple than to the complex end of the spectrum, but he is not, like many of the stereotypes of boys' fiction, an absolutely simple character. Although he unswervingly pursues a single goal throughout the novel, and is in this respect a simple character, he is capable at least of some hesitation, self-doubt, internal division, and therefore tends towards complexity. In the same novel, Ishmael and Starbuck are more complex than Ahab, yet neither is equal in complexity to Becky Sharp and Rawdon Crawley. Complexity, then, is a matter of degree; a character may be more or less complex.

FUNCTION OF COMPLEX CHARACTERS: Should a writer choose complexity or simplicity in the portrayal of character? It is often suggested (by Forster, among others) that the complex, or round, character is a higher kind of achievement than the simple. As we shall see, this view must be seriously qualified. But let's begin by examining the functions that can best be served by the complex character.

COMPLEXITY AND RELEVANCE: Complex characters are more lifelike than simple characters and, as we have seen, lifelikeness is one form of relevance. No real human being can be adequately summed up in a formula, as a simple character can. Certainly no reader of fiction would be willing to admit that he can be so summed up. Real human beings are capable of surprising us. The complex character can surprise us; the simple character cannot. We may conclude, then, that complexity of character tends to produce lifelikeness in the work of fiction.

COMPLEXITY AND CRAFTSMANSHIP: There is another basis for the admiration critics often express for the well-drawn complex character. As an achievement in literary craftsmanship, the complex character is in many ways more difficult than the simple. The simple character need only repeat his basic formula each time he appears on the scene. Revealing a character's complexity to the reader, on the other hand, is an immensely complicated business. Complexity cannot be achieved at the price of coherence, however. It is not enough that the complex character not have a formula, that he act differently at different points in the story. The complexity we want is the complexity of a unified character. The writer must, then, satisfy simultaneously our demand for complexity and our demand for unity. This is why writers are condemned for letting their personages behave "out of character," that is, in a manner inconsistent with what we know of them. To behave in this way lends a character complexity, perhaps, but at the cost of unity. If we did not feel that Rawdon Crawley of the early scenes of *Vanity Fair* was capable of becoming the Rawdon Crawley of the later scenes, he would be a failure as a character. It is the combination of complexity and unity, the sense of unity in complexity, that is impressive.

CONSISTENCY: It may be objected at this point that, since human beings often act inconsistently, there is no reason to demand unity of fictional characters. There are several possible answers to this objection. First, it is not certain that human beings do really act inconsistently. The apparent inconsistencies of human behavior may simply indicate the limits of our knowledge of ourselves and others. Seen in the right perspective, in the eye of God or the psychoanalyst for example, we may all behave more consistently than we know.

But we need not retreat to metaphysics or psychoanalysis to settle this problem. We need only remind ourselves once again that the fictional character, however complex, is not a human being. He is himself an artistic creation, part of an artistic whole. And we traditionally demand of art a sense of form we do not find in life. This sense of form is, in fact, probably the essential difference between art and life. Briefly, when we praise a literary character for being lifelike, we should remember that this is not an adjective we would apply to a human being. A thing cannot be lifelike unless it is really not alive.

Finally, it may be pointed out that the writer of fiction can depict inconsistency in human behavior. But, as Aristotle advises in his *Poetics,* if a character is to be inconsistent, let him be consistently inconsistent. Inconsistency should not be something the writer resorts to simply to get him out of plot difficulties, as when the wicked uncle has a change of heart in the last chapter in order that the story may come to an otherwise impossible, and still incredible, happy ending.

FUNCTIONS OF SIMPLE CHARACTERS: Consistency should be no problem with simple characters, for the simple character is by definition consistent. What many readers object to in simple characters is that they are consistent at the price of complexity, and their lack of complexity violates our sense of the human personality. There is some truth in this charge, but we must recognize that the simple character can perform many important functions in the work of fiction.

SIMPLICITY AND LIFELIKENESS: We have said that, because human beings are complex, complex characters are more lifelike than simple characters. Now we must see that simple characters can make an important contribution to the overall lifelikeness of a work of fiction.

The fact is, if I think of my life as a story, I find it contains more simple than complex characters. Does this contradict what has been said about the complexity of the human personality? Not really. Again, it's a matter of perspective.

In the story of my life, I am the most complex character. This doesn't mean that I am really more complex than other people, but that I am more aware of my own complexities than I am of theirs. I know myself from the inside, others only from the outside.

Still, among the "others," there are some I know quite well. These include my immediate family and my closest friends. I can't know them as well as I know myself, but I can be aware of some of their complexities.

And then there are the other "others," ranging from casual acquaintances to people I pass in the street. In the eye of God, no doubt, each of these is a highly complex personality, but in my eyes they are simple characters. Whatever complexity they may have I know little or nothing about.

And this brings us to the connection between the simple character and lifelikeness. The use of simple characters to fulfill minor roles in a work of fiction satisfies my sense of life, not perhaps as it really is (the eye of God, again), but as I experience it. The simple character, then, can serve very well as a minor character in fiction, contributing, as we have seen, to our sense of the overall lifelikeness of the story.

SIMPLICITY AND IMAGINATION: But the simple character is not limited in fiction to use as a minor character, part of the background against which the main action is played out. As we have seen, Captain Ahab, protagonist of Melville's *Moby Dick*, is essentially a simple character, as are many of the principal characters in Dickens. Is a writer justified in making major characters simple?

We must first of all distinguish again between the stereotyped simple character (the poor but honest working girl) and the individualized simple character (Ahab, Uriah Heep). Stereotypes are substitutes for imagination; the individualized simple character is an original imaginative creation. Except in very special circumstances, stereotypes will appear as major characters only in fiction of a very low order. But the individualized simple character may be an imaginative accomplishment worthy to take a central position in fiction of the very highest order.

Again, we must remind ourselves that relevance, rather than lifelikeness, is the important standard. Ahab is not lifelike. I have never met anyone like him, and I trust I never shall. But in Ahab's total commitment to an obsession, I recognize a part of myself. That is the secret of his relevance, of his power. That is why, in spite of his relative simplicity, he can stand at the very center of a major work of fiction.

We may make a few tentative generalizations. Insofar as the author's end is realism, the accurate presentation of the surface of life, we may expect that his principal characters will be complex. The simple character is the more likely to appear in a major role as the writer drifts away from realism. Thackeray, the realist, gives us complex characters, while Melville, the symbolic romancer, gives us a simple character as protagonist. Finally, that kind of simple character we call the stereotype may appear in a minor role in serious fiction, but will play a major part, as a general rule, only in inferior fiction.

EVALUATION OF CHARACTER TYPES: It is, then, an oversimplification to assert without qualification that the complex character is a greater achievement than the simple. If we think of character in itself, divorced from the other elements of fiction, we may place a high value on complexity. But if we examine character in the light of the story as a whole, we must see that complexity is not necessarily a greater virtue than simplicity. We must always ask what the character contributes to the story. And the author must always choose the kind of character appropriate to his overall purpose.

METHODS OF CHARACTER PORTRAYAL

The author must choose not only what kind of characters he will present, but also by what methods he will present them. There are a number of methods available to the author, each with its advantages and disadvantages. We shall classify these as the discursive, the dramatic, and the contextual.

DISCURSIVE METHOD: The author who chooses the discursive method simply tells us about his characters. He enumerates their qualities and may even express approval or disapproval of them. The advantages of this method are simplicity and economy. The writer who is content to tell us directly about his characters can quickly finish the job of characterization and go on to other things.

This method, like the others, has its disadvantages. It is relatively mechanical and discourages the reader's imaginative participation. That is, the reader is not encouraged to react directly to the characters, to make up his own mind about them, as he must react to and make up his own mind about the real people he meets.

Modern writers and critics have tended to regard the discursive method of characterization as intrinsically inferior to other methods. The author, according to this view, should not tell us, he should show us. Like most critical generalizations, this one oversimplifies. The discursive method can be the best choice under certain circumstances. When economy and directness are desired, the author may well consider the discursive method.

THE DRAMATIC METHOD: Economy and directness are always virtues, but they are not always the virtues appropriate to the situation. Therefore, the discursive method will not always serve. The principal alternative to the discursive method is the dramatic method, the method of showing rather than telling.

In the dramatic method, the author allows his characters to reveal themselves to us through their own words and actions. This, of course, is how character is revealed to us in drama; that is why we call this method dramatic. But it is also how people reveal themselves to us in life. In life, there is no author around to tell us that Mr. X is generous. Rather, by observing what Mr. X does and what he says, we may conclude that Mr. X is generous. It is the same with the fictional character presented dramatically.

The advantages of the dramatic method should be obvious. Compared to the discursive method, the dramatic is more life-like and invites the reader's active participation in the story. The dramatic method has been generally favored by writers of fiction in the twentieth century.

This method has its disadvantages. It is less economical than the discursive, since to show takes longer than to tell. And, while it encourages the reader's active participation, it also increases the possibility of his misjudging the character. This second difficulty should, of course, not exist for the alert reader, provided the author has been sufficiently skillful in his showing. When vividness of presentation is more important than economy, the writer will choose the dramatic method.

CHARACTERS ON OTHER CHARACTERS: Included under the general heading of the dramatic method is the device of having one character in a story talk about another. The reader must remember, of course, that information received in this way is not necessarily reliable. What A says of B may tell us more about A than about B. Still, this is one source of information about character.

THE CONTEXTUAL METHOD: By the contextual method we mean the device of suggesting character by the verbal context that surrounds the character. If, for instance, a character is constantly described in terms appropriate to a beast of prey, the reader may well conclude that the author is trying to tell him something.

MIXING METHODS: The reader will rarely find a work of fiction in which only one of the methods outlined above is employed. Indeed, the contextual method can be used effectively only in combination with other methods. In evaluating an author's methods of characterization, the reader must keep in mind the appropriateness of the author's methods to the overall design of the story.

REVELATION AND DEVELOPMENT: Up to this point, we have been talking about character and the methods of portraying it as if the author's job were simply to show the character to us and then go into other things. But the revelation of character may be only part of the author's concern; he may also be interested in the development of character. In Thackeray's portrayal of Rawdon Crawley, for instance, development is of the greatest importance. Development, of course, implies the passage of time. Thus we may expect a greater emphasis on development of character in the novel, since the novel permits the author to show the passage of time more fully, while the short story will often concentrate on the revelation of character.

MOTIVATION: We have insisted throughout this discussion that character must always be seen as one element in a larger artistic whole. The point at which character and plot come together is what we mean by the term motivation. Plot, for the most part, consists of what the characters do. Motivation is why they do it.

We may think of motivation as general or particular. General motivation covers such basic human drives as love, hunger, greed, and so on. Particular motivation involves the individual applications of these basic drives. If the hero acts to impress the heroine, this is particular motivation, an application of such general motives as love and, perhaps, vanity. It is part of coherence in character and plot that the reader be able to identify both the general and particular motivation for the actions of the characters. It is part of the story's general plausibility that the motivation be at all times adequate to the action. If a character kills, we should be satisfied that we know why he killed and that the "why" is an adequate reason, or at least would seem adequate to the character, to act as he does.

CONCLUSION: In the present chapter we have, of necessity, talked much of character and only occasionally of the relation of character to the story as a whole. It must be recognized that this kind of discussion can be misleading unless we keep in mind the artificiality of the distinction, for instance, between character and plot.

We should note further that character is not essential to fiction in the same way that plot is. Without plot, fiction is impossible; it is, on the other hand, possible for fiction to get by without what most of us would recognize as character.

We can still recognize, however, that an individual writer may choose to stress either plot or character. For writers who stress character, the main function, perhaps the only function, of plot is to serve the revelation or development of character. But whether an individual author's primary interest is in plot or in character, it is the ability of the author to blend the two into a seamless unity that is the mark of his genius.

CHAPTER 3

SETTING

INTRODUCTION: Everything that happens happens somewhere at some time. That element of fiction which reveals to us the where and when of events we call setting. In other words, the term "setting" refers to the point in time and space at which the events of the plot occur. The setting of George Eliot's *Middlemarch,* for instance, is an English town in the nineteenth century, that of Ernest Hemingway's *The Sun Also Rises* includes Paris, Pamplona, and several other spots in France and Spain during the 1920's.

TYPES OF SETTINGS

NEUTRAL SETTINGS: Often the setting in a work of fiction is little more than a reflection of the truth that things have to happen somewhere. The author's principal concern is with plot or character, and he sketches in only enough of the setting to lend the requisite verisimilitude to the action. Most of the fiction in popular magazines, for instance, has a vaguely contemporary setting, either urban or rural. Beyond giving us this much information, the author has no real interest in his setting and does not encourage such interest on our part. When this is true, we may speak of the setting of the story as "neutral."

The use of the neutral setting is by no means limited to slick commercial fiction. Henry Fielding's *Tom Jones,* certainly one of the great novels in English, reveals little positive interest in setting. An inn is an inn, Fielding seems to believe, and a barnyard is a barnyard. There is no reason to single out whatever qualities may make the inns and barnyards in one part of England different from their counterparts in other parts of the country.

Limits to Neutrality: Even in the work of a writer like Fielding, however, the neutrality of the setting is not absolute. If his inns are typical inns and his barnyards typical barnyards, still he recognizes that some scenes are properly set in inns, others in barnyards. He recognizes, that is, the value of a certain appropriateness of setting to event.

The same is true in modern commercial fiction. If a story in one of the monthly women's magazines has a rural setting, this sets up in the reader certain expectations regarding character and plot. To be sure, these expectations are often based on the crudest sort of stereotypes. Nevertheless, they indicate that an absolutely neutral setting is rare.

THE SPIRITUAL SETTING: The expectations aroused in us by a rural setting suggest that few settings are absolutely neutral, because few settings are merely physical. For the modern American reader, a rural setting suggests not just grass, cows, and barns, but certain values which must be called spiritual. As long as the setting is only vaguely and conventionally rural, the values suggested are likely to be vague and conventional as well. But as the physical setting becomes more specific and more vividly rendered, so does the spiritual setting.

By the spiritual setting, then, we mean the values embodied in or implied by the physical setting. The phrase "a small midwestern town" may immediately suggest one set of values, while New York City suggests quite another. That this is not only true in fiction but extends beyond fiction may be seen from a recent court case. A judge awarded custody of a child to the child's grandparents on the grounds that the grandparents were "good, midwestern people." Apparently the term "midwestern" had for the judge a spiritual as well as geographical significance.

Refining the Spiritual Setting: We would hardly expect a writer of any merit to accept the judge's easy identification of the midwestern with the virtuous. This is precisely the kind of stereotype the serious writer will seek to avoid. He will also, of course, seek to avoid the kind of reverse stereotype which would make of "midwestern" a term of abuse.

The serious writer will recognize, and will force us to recognize, that there is no easy relationship between a particular physical setting and virtue or vice. He will, by precise observation and careful rendering, refine the setting until we are aware of the complex of conflicting values that may inhere in a particular place and time. George Eliot's portrayal of life in a Victorian English town in her novel *Middlemarch* is one of the highest achievements of this sort in English fiction.

SETTING AS DYNAMIC: What has been said should indicate that setting need not mean merely a static backdrop before which the action unfolds itself. Setting may thrust itself dynamically into the action, affecting events and being in turn affected by them, until setting seems to assume the role of a major character.

Our original definition of setting as a point in time and space therefore needs some development. For time and space are not themselves neutral. To be born into one century rather than another, in one region rather than another, can have the profoundest effects on every aspect of a person's life. The same attitude may mark a man as a rebel in one generation, a reactionary in the next; a hero in one country, a traitor in another.

THE ELEMENTS OF SETTING: What are the elements of which setting is composed? They may be listed under four headings: (1) the actual geographical location, including topography, scenery, even the details of a room's interior; (2) the occupations and modes of day-to-day existence of the characters; (3) the time in which the action takes place, e.g., historical period, season of the year; (4) the religious, moral, intellectual, social, and emotional environment of the characters.

FUNCTIONS OF SETTING

SETTING AS METAPHOR: We have thus far been limiting our discussion to the literal presentation of setting. Even what we have called "spiritual setting" does not essentially involve a departure from the literal, since it extends only to the observable, if intangible, effects that time and place may have on character and events. Now we shall discuss a use of setting that involves extra-literal elements.

Sometimes in fiction we encounter details of setting that seem to function as a projection or objectification of the internal states of the characters or of a pervasive spiritual condition. For instance, the fog that lingers so oppressively in Charles Dickens' *Bleak House* serves as a kind of metaphor for the spiritual malaise and confusion of the characters. This is not the same as what we call the spiritual setting. It is not the fog that has contributed to the characters' malaise. If anything, it is the other way around.

But not quite, of course. Only in fantasy could a writer ask us to believe that a character's internal state could create an external fog. The fog in *Bleak House* is as truly there as the town in *Middlemarch*. But George Eliot asks us to observe the spiritual and emotional effects of the town on the individual, while Dickens asks us to see the fog as a metaphor (i.e., an implied comparison) for the individual's spiritual and emotional state.

ATMOSPHERE: A further function of setting, related to but not identical with its metaphorical function, is the creation of atmosphere. Atmosphere has been more talked about than defined, and, because it refers to the suggested rather than the stated, it may be impossible to define satisfactorily. One critic has described it as the air breathed by the reader as he enters the world of the literary work. It is a kind of mood or emotional aura suggested primarily by the setting and helping to establish the reader's expectations. A suggestion of mystery and fore-boding may be established, for instance, by a description of shapes dimly seen in the darkness. A stormy night carries with it one emotional aura, a sunny morning another.

The close relation that often exists between the function of setting in creating atmosphere and the function of setting as metaphor may be seen if we refer again to the fog of Dickens' *Bleak House*. We have seen that the fog serves as a metaphor for the spiritual and emotional state of the principal characters. But it also affects the reader; it is part of the air he breathes as he enters the world of Dickens' novel. And as such it contributes to the creation of atmosphere.

We should note the possibility of contrast in atmosphere. A cheerful atmosphere created by a bright, sunlit setting may contrast with the inner disturbance of a character. Or there may be contrasting atmospheres in the same story. Our increasing sense of foreboding as the hero walks into the darkening forest in Hawthorne's "Young Goodman Brown" is an example of a gradual and subtle shift in atmosphere.

SETTING AS THE DOMINANT ELEMENT: Like character, setting may be the element of primary importance in a particular story or even in the work of a particular author. Certainly George Eliot's *Middlemarch* setting, particularly the spiritual setting, strikes us as at least as important as plot and character. In this novel, and others like it, plot and character seem to exist primarily as a means of revealing the effects of setting on human life.

TIME AS THE DOMINANT ELEMENT: In many works of fiction, the time in which the action occurs is of the highest importance. This is especially true of historical fiction, like William Makepeace Thackeray's *Henry Esmond* or Charles Dickens' *A Tale of Two Cities.* In the latter novel, the French Revolution and the terror that followed it affect the lives of all the characters.

The customs and moral conventions of a particular time, part of the spiritual setting, may be of great importance even in works of fiction that are not intentionally historical. Thomas Hardy gave his *Jude the Obscure* a contemporary setting; that is, he set it in his own period. Still, it is Jude's inability to find personal fulfillment within the moral framework, the spiritual setting, of that particular period that is the basis of his tragedy. The modern reader may even be more aware than Hardy of the important role time plays in this novel.

That the particular terms of a moral conflict, like the one in *Jude the Obscure,* are related to a particular period does not necessarily mean that the work dramatizing this conflict lacks universality. The pattern of frustrated rebellion depicted in *Jude the Obscure* is itself universal, although it takes different forms in different generations.

We should perhaps make a special note of works of fiction in which temporal setting takes on added importance with the passage of time. Ernest Hemingway's *The Sun Also Rises* and F. Scott Fitzgerald's *The Great Gatsby* were written in the 1920's about the 1920's. In the years since World War II, this period has had a special fascination for readers. One result is that novels like these two have taken on for modern readers a particular significance as portraits of their period, an interest that could not have been felt in the same way by those who read the novels when they first appeared. More recently, novels of the 1930's such as those of Henry Roth and Daniel Fuchs seem to be arousing a similar interest.

PLACE AS THE DOMINANT ELEMENT: Works of fiction in which the spatial setting, or place, dominates are generally classified as examples of local color or regionalism. The regionalist seeks to investigate the effects on character of a particular geographical setting—which means, of course, a spiritual as well as physical setting.

The regionalist's interest in what it is like to live in a particular place—say, the deep South—is not in any sense a rejection of universality. The process of being influenced by the region in which one is born and raised is a universal process. Moreover, we may well discern within the particular *mores* of a particular place further patterns of behavior that are universal.

A number of important writers of fiction have devoted all or most of their work in fiction to the depiction of life in a particular region. Among English novelists, Thomas Hardy is distinguished for his novels of Wessex. In *The Return of the Native,* one of his most famous novels, Hardy makes of Egden Heath a force more powerful than any of the human figures in the story. The United States has produced distinguished regionalists as well. Willa Cather deals extensively with life on the Nebraska prairie in such works as *My Antonia*; George Washington Cable's *The Grandissimes* is an important novel of Southern life in the nineteenth century; Sarah Orne Jewett and Mary Wilkins Freeman are among the most significant writers of fiction devoted to life in New England.

The names mentioned above are only a few of the important regionalists of England and the United States. Other nations have, of course, produced their regionalists as well. The writers we call regionalists differ among themselves in many ways. But they all share the desire to render the authentic qualities of particular places. The greatest of them, like Hardy, seek as well to discover the universal in the particular. The power of the regionalists' best work indicates clearly the positive contribution setting can make to literary art.

The nineteenth-century English writer Anthony Trollope and the twentieth-century American William Faulkner are regionalists of a special sort. Each has created an imaginary region as a setting for his fiction. Barsetshire, the setting of such novels as *The Warden* and *Barchester Towers* by Trollope, and Yoknapatawpha County, setting of many of Faulkner's works, will not be found on any map. Barsetshire is a composite picture of many English counties, while Yoknapatawpha is based on the actual county in Mississippi where Faulkner lived much of his life. Both Trollope and Faulkner share the regionalists' concern for the effect of setting on character and incident.

SETTING IN NONREALISTIC FICTION: The reader may be disturbed to note that most of what has been said of setting applies to fiction in a more or less realistic mode. What of setting in such *genres* as fantasy and science fiction? In fact, no specific discussion of setting in these *genres* is necessary. In fantastic as in realistic fiction, setting may serve the functions we have been discussing and may range, like the settings of realistic fiction, from the neutral to the vital and essential. In short, what has been said of setting in realistic fiction applies as well to setting in nonrealistic fiction.

SETTING AND THE WHOLE STORY: We have seen that setting may be the dominant element in a work of fiction. Still, setting never exists by itself. It is always part of an artistic whole and must be understood as such. Some readers turn to fiction out of a fascination with character. Certainly fiction can satisfy such an interest, but an interest in character divorced from the other elements of fiction is a psychological rather than a literary interest. Some readers may turn to fiction for what it can tell them of other times and other places. This too is a legitimate interest in itself and one that fiction can satisfy. But an interest in setting divorced from the other elements of fiction is a historical or sociological, not a literary, interest. A literary interest will always concentrate on the whole work.

In evaluation, then, we have a right to demand vividness in the presentation of setting. But the vividness we should demand is that appropriate to the story as a whole. A vivid description of a setting may be an artistic flaw if it destroys the overall design of the work. For in the best fiction the rendering of setting is never an end in itself. Rather, setting must be one element in a unified artistic whole, and we must ask of setting as of character, not only what interest it has in itself, but also what it contributes to the complex whole that is the work of fiction.

CHAPTER 4

POINT OF VIEW

INTRODUCTION: Few topics have received more attention from serious modern critics of fiction than point of view. And not only the critics but writers of fiction themselves have been especially drawn in this century to a consideration of this topic; one need only consult the essays of Henry James for an illustration. One might even conclude from a study of critical pronouncements on the subject that the choice of point of view is the most important single choice the writer of fiction makes.

At the same time, the average casual reader, the kind of reader who turns to fiction for pleasure in his leisure time, hardly seems aware of the issues involved in the choice of point of view. It is not an exaggeration to say that the very term "point of view" is either unfamiliar to, or misunderstood by, the average non-professional, non-scholarly reader of fiction.

All the same it seems clear that, whether consciously or not, the average unreflective reader is affected by point of view and that, whether or not it is the most important choice he must make, the choice of point of view is one to which the writer of fiction must give careful attention.

If this is so, then we had first better be sure that we know what we mean by point of view. One of the problems we face is that the expression "point of view" has several meanings besides the limited, technical one it has in the critical analysis of fiction. In fact my awareness of this problem led me to consider seriously the possibility of using some other term for this topic. But I finally decided that, since this is the term most commonly used, I would only be inviting confusion by introducing another.

DEFINING POINT OF VIEW

WHAT POINT OF VIEW IS NOT: It may be best to begin by distinguishing the meaning of point of view in literary terms from other meanings that may be assigned to the same phrase. If you are asked for your point of view on a subject, what do you understand by the request? Chances are, you conclude you're being asked to express your opinions or attitudes. This is, at least, one sense of point of view. It is not, however, the sense we have in mind when we speak of point of view in fiction.

AN ANALOGY: Let's try an analogy. Let's compare point of view in fiction with point of view in purely physical terms. If I stand directly in front of you, I can't see your shoulder blades. If I want to see your shoulder blades, one of us has to move. That is, I have to look at you from another point of view.

In short, from any single physical point of view, there are some things I can see, and some things I can not.

THE EYEWITNESS: Now let's imagine that an accident has occurred, two cars have collided. There are four eyewitnesses to the accident. An investigating officer questions the witnesses. He also questions the drivers of the two cars and a passenger who was in one of the cars. He questions seven people in all.

And he finds that he has seven quite different accounts of what happened.

Let's make clear that nobody is lying. Each person is telling the truth to the best of his ability. Why, then, don't their stories coincide in all details? Because each is speaking from his own point of view.

When we say this, we mean in part that each person saw the accident from a different point of view in physical terms. One witness was on one side of the street, another on the other side, and so on. But we mean a little more. A witness who just happened to be passing by is not involved in the accident in the same way that the drivers are. Relatively speaking, the passerby's involvement is rather remote. The passenger is certainly more immediately involved than a casual onlooker. But he is not involved in the same way as the driver, either.

Whose story is likely to be most reliable? Well, the drivers were most directly involved, but their very involvement may make them unreliable because they can't be entirely objective. A passerby would probably be more objective, but might have observed less. The passenger's account would be useful but limited.

In short, no single account could be expected to tell the whole story, yet each will provide something that the others lack. The only account that could give the whole story is God's, and that is not likely to be available.

THE AUTHOR'S POWER: In fiction, however, something like a Godlike view of things can be available. For the author's relation to the world he creates in fiction is, after all, similar to God's relation to His created universe. That is, the author is the ultimate source of being of every person, place, thing, and event in his work and knows all there is to know about these creatures of his imagination. But he must decide whether he will exploit his special knowledge. He must, that is, find the point of view most appropriate to the story he wants to tell.

POSSIBLE POINTS OF VIEW

FIRST PERSON OR THIRD PERSON?:   A story may be told from the inside or the outside. When we speak of a story told from the inside, we mean a story told by one of the participants or characters in the story. Stories told from the inside are spoken of as examples of first-person narration, since the narrator naturally uses the first personal pronoun "I" in referring to himself. Stories told from the outside, by a usually nameless narrator who may be more or less closely identified with the author, are spoken of as examples of third-person narration, since the narrator will rarely refer to himself at all (exceptions are found mainly in novels of the eighteenth and nineteenth centuries) and refers to the characters of the story in the third person.

OMNISCIENT OR LIMITED?: The distinction between first-person and third-person narration is commonly made and has its uses. But distinction based merely on grammatical form is likely in itself to be superficial. (We shall see, however, that this apparently superficial distinction may have significant implications.) A still more basic distinction is that between omniscient and limited narration.

THE OMNISCIENT NARRATOR: The author who chooses to exploit his Godlike knowledge of the fictional universe he has created will employ the omniscient narrator. Within the framework of the work of fiction, the omniscient narrator knows, simply, everything. He can at will enter the mind of any character and tell the reader directly what the character is thinking. He can at one moment be in the city, at the next in the country. In one paragraph he can be with us in the present, in the next he can take us into the past. The only motive required for his moves from mind to mind, from place to place, from time to time, is the desire to tell the story as well as possible.

Thackeray's *Vanity Fair* is one of the classic examples in English fiction of the use of the omniscient narrator. Thackeray carries this technique very far indeed, for his narrator not only knows everything about the people and events of the story; he knows a good deal about the world in general as well and frequently interrupts the narrative for the purpose of introducing, sometimes seriously, sometimes ironically, bits of moral or philosophical reflection.

Such interruptions are not a necessary part of the technique of omniscient narration. They are seldom to be found in more modern novels using this technique. For the mark of the omniscient narrator is not his philosophizing, but his faculty of knowing all.

The omniscient technique is essentially a third-person technique. Even when, as in *Vanity Fair,* the narrator occasionally refers to himself in the first person, the characters in the story he narrates remain firmly in the third person.

The Advantages of Omniscience: In a sense, omniscient narration is the most natural of all narrative techniques. After all, the author is, with regard to his work, omniscient. Any pretense to limitations on his knowledge of the characters he has himself created is clearly artificial. And because omniscient narration is the most natural form, it may be for many writers the most comfortable form.

In addition, omniscient narration is a highly flexible technique. As we have suggested, in omniscient narration, there are virtually no limits to what the omniscient narrator can tell us. He can always give us just what the story demands and need have no other concern.

The Disadvantages of Omniscience: Although omniscient narration is, in one sense, a particularly natural technique, it is in another sense an especially unnatural one. For in life, after 'all, there are no omniscient people. The narrator who knows and tells as much as he likes is purely a convention of literature. For those who regard "naturalness" as a virtue in literature, then, omniscience is not always the most desirable technique.

Furthermore, the very flexibility of omniscient narration, while certainly a virtue in itself, can present problems. In the hands of an insufficiently disciplined writer, omniscient narration can tend to looseness and incoherence, since the technique does not impose discipline on a writer.

LIMITED NARRATION: The alternative to the omniscient narrator is the limited narrator. As has been implied, limited narration is always artificial, since there are in truth no limits to an author's knowledge of his own creation. Still, art is in part a matter of artifice, and the artifice of limited narration offers a number of advantages to the writer of fiction. It also has its disadvantages, of course, and we shall examine some of them as well.

THE NARRATOR: The limited narrator is, simply, a narrator who doesn't know everything. He may appear both in stories told from the inside (first-person narration) and in stories told from the outside (third-person narration). It is when we turn to the limited narrator that the matter of point of view begins to take on major importance. In a sense, the omniscient author has no point of view. Able to observe the action from all sides at once, and not personally involved in it, he simply sees things as they are—at least, as they are in the imaginary world of the story.

Protagonist as Narrator: The omniscient narrator, like God, has no point of view. But characters, like people, have points of view. And when the story is told, not by an omniscient narrator serenely and disinterestedly viewing the action from above, but by one of the characters, then we may clearly say the story is told from a particular point of view.

The story may be told, for instance, by the protagonist or main character. In that case, it is told from his point of view. We see only what he sees, and we see it only as he sees it.

The use of the protagonist as narrator has certain obvious advantages. It corresponds very closely to the reader's experience of life, for each of us is the protagonist in a first-person story. Like the narrator-protagonist we know ourselves from the inside, others only from the outside. I know my own thoughts directly. The thoughts of others I must infer from their words and actions. Therefore, the use of the protagonist as narrator, telling his own story in the first person, has the advantages of immediacy and the sense of life.

A further advantage of this method is that it can make a positive contribution to the overall unity of the work. That he must include in his story only what the narrator can be expected to know gives the author a valuable principle of selection and helps him to avoid the looseness sometimes associated with omniscient narration.

The advantages of telling the story from the point of view of the protagonist suggest some of the disadvantages connected with the method. What in some stories may be a source of immediacy, intensity, and unity can in others be simply an unfortunate restriction. The author may be frustrated to find that he can include in the story only what his narrator may be expected to know. If he has chosen his point of view unwisely, the author may resort excessively to tricks for introducing additional information. He may, for instance, rely too heavily on letters, telephone calls, and conversations between his protagonist-narrator and other characters to convey information. All of these devices are legitimate in themselves, but excessive reliance on them becomes too obviously a mechanical solution to a technical problem, distracting our attention from the story to the author's difficulties in writing it.

There are also problems that arise from the fact that in a story told by the protagonist we are in a sense locked within the mind of the protagonist. This is not in itself a flaw, but it suggests that this method may not be suitable to all subjects. For instance, moral judgment of the protagonist is difficult to handle in a story told by the protagonist, unless the reader can be convinced that the protagonist is more given than most of us to self-analysis and self-evaluation. Even Henry James, one of the masters of point of view, fails in his story "The Aspern Papers" to solve the problem of how to incorporate a moral attitude towards the protagonist into a story told by the protagonist. We are left, in this generally remarkable story, with the sense that James has tried to make this point of view do more than it can.

Protagonist as Viewpoint Character: Closely related to the point of view we have been discussing is that associated with "third-person limited" narration. In this technique the story is told from the outside by a narrator who, like the omniscient narrator, is not himself a character in the story he narrates. But in the third-person limited technique, the narrator is not omniscient. In the form of third-person limited we are now concerned with, the narrator knows all there is to know about one character. Beyond that, he knows only what this one character knows. The controlling point of view is that of the character, who is therefore referred to by critics as the viewpoint character.

The viewpoint character may be the protagonist, in which case this method is very close to the first-person technique discussed above. The principal difference is that in the first-person technique narrator and protagonist are one and the same, while in the third-person technique they remain clearly distinguished.

This difference has important implications. The narrator in a third-person limited story is always more or less detached from the viewpoint character. This detachment presents an opportunity for kinds of irony, evaluation, interpretation not possible in first-person narration. Consider, for instance, the following brief passage from Henry James's novel *The Ambassadors*. "Strether" is Lambert Strether, the novel's protagonist and viewpoint character:

> Many things came over him, and one of them was that he should doubtless presently know whether he had been shallow or sharp. Another was that the balcony in question didn't somehow show as a convenience easy to surrender. Poor Strether had at this very moment to recognize the truth that, wherever one paused in Paris, the imagination, before one could stop it, reacted.

There is nothing in the first two sentences of this passage that could not, with the necessary changes in grammatical form, be included in a story told in the first person. But at the word "Poor," the first word in the third sentence, narrator and viewpoint character part company. "Poor" is the narrator's comment on the viewpoint character, and this kind of comment is, of course, impossible in first-person narration.

Apart from this important distinction, the two points of view have much in common and share many of the same advantages and disadvantages. In third-person limited, the author must restrict himself to what might be known by his viewpoint character, and this can be either a valuable discipline or a frustrating restriction, depending on the temperament of the author and the nature of his material.

Minor Character Viewpoint: The character selected as narrator or viewpoint character need not be the protagonist. These roles may also be assumed by characters of lesser importance. Minor character viewpoint obviously has many of the same advantages and disadvantages as major character viewpoint, whether first-person or third-person limited. There is the additional problem that telling the story from the point of view of a minor character requires a special sort of justification. If a story is at all interesting, the protagonist's point of view should be interesting, since he is the central character in the story. But what makes a minor character's point of view interesting? The answer must be that his point of view allows us to see facets of the situation that we would otherwise miss. In *The Great Gatsby,* for instance, the narrator's ambiguous relation to the sophisticated society of East Egg makes him an especially perceptive and valuable commentator on the action of the novel.

Objective Viewpoint: An external instance of limited narration occurs when the narrator is not permitted to know directly the thoughts of any of the characters. He can observe only what becomes external in word and action. This technique is sometimes referred to as the objective viewpoint (some critics prefer the term "dramatic"). A striking instance of the objective viewpoint maintained with unusual rigor throughout an entire story is Ernest Hemingway's "The Killers"; Hemingway is in general a master of the objective viewpoint.

Given the right kind of subject, as in "The Killers," the objective viewpoint can have great force. But its refusal to deal directly with the inner life is a serious limitation, since it is thus obviously not suited to many of the subjects great writers of fiction have considered most important.

COMBINATIONS: The basic points of view in fiction, then, are the omniscient and the limited. The limited may involve either first or third-person narration; the narrator or viewpoint character may be either a major or minor character in the story; an extreme form of the limited point of view is the so-called objective viewpoint.

Now these different points of view may appear in combination in the same story. In fact, a work of fiction that is as a whole an example of omniscient narration will usually include all or most of the other points of view as well. That is, at some point in his narrative, the omniscient narrator will simply describe externals and will therefore be assuming the objective viewpoint. At another moment, the narrator will present a scene to us from the point of view of one of the characters and will therefore employ third-person limited narration.

MULTIPLE VIEWPOINTS: Not to be confused with a combination of different point of view techniques is the use of multiple viewpoints, which is actually a particular application of the limited point of view. An important example is William Faulkner's novel *As I Lay Dying*. Part by part, Faulkner's consistent use of the limited point of view is clear. At any given moment in the novel the action is being seen from the point of view of a single character. We see only what that character sees and as that character sees it. But the novel as a whole contains no less than sixteen viewpoint characters; we see the action from the point of view of each one in turn.

A variation on the use of multiple viewpoints is the so-called epistolary novel, the novel made up entirely of letters written by the characters. Samuel Richardson's *Clarissa Harlowe* and Tobias Smollett's *Humphrey Clinker* are two of the greatest English epistolary novels.

POINT OF VIEW AND MEANING: Treated in isolation from the other elements of literature, point of view may seem to the inexperienced reader a narrowly technical concern. After all, it may be objected, it's the story that counts and not the point of view from which it is told.

But this objection is unsound, for story and point of view are not truly distinct entities. Would the same story, told from another point of view, be just as good? The truth seems to be that you can't tell the same story from another point of view. Change the point of view and you change the story.

Imagine "The Killers" retold as a first-person story with Ole as protagonist and narrator. Would it still be the same story? Surely not. Nor would *The Great Gatsby* be the same story if it were told by an uninvolved omniscient narrator, rather than by the sensitive and sympathetic Nick.

And when we come to works like *As I Lay Dying* or Lawrence Durrell's *Alexandria Quartet,* it seems almost fair to say that the point of view is the story. That is, it is precisely our awareness of the different shapes experience can assume in different minds that suggests the central meaning of such works.

Some writers have even used point of view to dramatize failures of understanding. In Ford Madox Ford's novel *The Good*

Soldier, the protagonist-narrator is unable to understand the events he relates. And his inability to find meaning in his experience is precisely the point, the meaning if you will, of the novel.

The choice of one point of view over another may have moral or philosophical meaning in itself. The writer who turns to the limited point of view may by his choice be expressing, whether consciously or not, his doubts of the possibility of ever knowing anything as it is in itself, independent of the point of view from which it is seen.

POINT OF VIEW AND CHOICE: We return once again to the theme of choice. You have been invited throughout this book to regard the work of fiction as a complex but unified form determined by a series of choices made by the author in the process of composition. In truth, the author is always omniscient. But he may choose, for the sake of his story to act as though he were not omniscient. And this choice, as much as any other made by the writer of fiction, has formal, moral, and philosophical significance. It is, then, not "merely a matter of technique" (whatever that may mean) but part of the meaning of fiction.

CHAPTER 5

STYLE AND TONE

INTRODUCTION: Although each of the topics discussed earlier in this book concerned us specifically as an element of fiction, no one of them is relevant only to fiction. Much of what we say of plot in fiction, for instance, is equally applicable to plot in drama.

At the same time no one of these topics is applicable to all forms of literature. There is, for instance, no "plot" in the usual sense in a lyric poem or essay.

The topics we shall discuss in this chapter, on the other hand, are qualities of all literary forms—one might almost say of all uses of language. Every literary work, at least, possesses the qualities of style and tone. What we shall be concerned with in this chapter is the particular relevance of style and tone to the analysis of fiction.

STYLE

RELATION OF STYLE TO TONE: As we shall see in the course of this chapter, the role of style in a work of fiction is an important and complex one. But none of the effects we may attribute to style is more important than its contribution to the establishment of tone. In this relationship we may regard style as the means, tone as the end. We shall first examine the nature of the means.

MEANING OF STYLE: We must first be aware that the term "style" has a number of meanings. When we speak of the "Attic style," for instance, we are speaking of a literary tendency that has flourished especially in some periods, but may be discovered in any period. On the other hand, there are "period styles," characteristic of one historical period and not to be found to any significant extent in any other.

We are more concerned with individual style, the single writer's way of using language, but we would be wise to remember that the full understanding of an individual writer's style may involve seeing that style in the context of the general style of his period and of recurrent literary tendencies. The style of the great English essayist Sir Francis Bacon, for example, may best be examined for its own qualities by one who can recognize its relation to the Attic style and to English prose of the later sixteenth and earlier seventeenth centuries in general.

Even when we have agreed our specific concern is with individual style, some ambiguities remain. If the complaint is made that a writer has no style, style seems to mean a generally desirable literary quality that some writers have, while others do not. If, on the other hand, we hear that Theodore Dreiser or James T. Farrell is an unsatisfactory stylist, we may conclude that all writers have style, but that not all styles are satisfactory.

Finally, if a critic undertakes an analysis of, say, Henry James's style, he may find evaluation impossible. After all, Henry James's style is undeniably Henry James's style. That is, style may simply mean a writer's characteristic way of using language. It is in this sense that all writers have style. And who can say that one man's style (say Dreiser's) is inferior to another's (say James's)? Isn't it possible, after all, that one style in this sense is never better or worse than another, but only different from it?

STYLE AND STANDARDS: The usual purposes of literary analysis demand that we be able to describe and to evaluate the material we are examining. To describe, first of all. It is then desirable that we isolate at once the particular qualities of a writer's style without attempting to judge either the individual qualities or the style as a whole. With a writer like Dreiser, for example, we must try to understand his style on its own terms, without being in too great a hurry to impose on it our notions of the kind of style we prefer. We should not condemn Dreiser simply because he is not Henry James. Neither, if our tastes tend in a different direction, should we condemn Henry James for not being Dreiser. A large part of this chapter will be devoted to suggesting methods and vocabulary that should be helpful in analyzing a writer's style on its own terms.

But in the discussion of literature, we always come at last to the act of judgment. A number of standards for evaluating style have been suggested at one time or another. For some critics economy is the supreme virtue; the writer must on no account use more words than are necessary. We may assent to this standard in a general way and still ask, "necessary to what?" Other critics prize concreteness above all else; yet we must recognize that the degree of concreteness in a given writer's style may quite properly be determined by the overall design of his work.

What we need, then, is a standard that will serve as a fairly useful guide and still remain flexible enough to prevent our condemning a writer for not achieving what he quite properly never attempted. The only standard I have ever found that meets these conditions is appropriateness; the style must be appropriate. If I am asked, "appropriate to what?" I can only answer, "To everything else in the work." Style, then, like every element of fiction, must ultimately be judged by its contribution to the artistic whole.

STYLE IS THE MAN: The assertion, "The style is the man," is commonly made in literary criticism. This assertion is relevant to our consideration of style in fiction. Part of our experience of the total work of fiction is our sense of the author, our awareness of and response to the qualities of his mind and personality. And the author reveals these qualities nowhere more clearly than in his style. For the choice of words and the arrangement of words into larger units such as the phrase, the sentence, the paragraph, are not merely mechanical processes. A writer's style can reveal to us his way of perceiving experience and of organizing his perceptions. The differences in style between a Dreiser and a James are ultimately differences of mind and personality.

But it may be objected that the style of many writers, including the authors of many best-selling novels and of stories in widely read magazines, is nothing more than a matter of formula. How can a formula reveal an individual writer's qualities of mind and personality? But doesn't one writer's willing submission to formula reveal such qualities as well as another writer's resistance to formula?

STYLE AND UNITY: Unity of style in itself may be sufficient to give total unity to a lyric poem or to a familiar essay, for in these forms the direct expression of a mind or personality is precisely what the work is all about. But fiction, although it may express the mind and personality of its author, does so indirectly. Making a plot is not, after all, a direct form of self-expression. Style alone, therefore, is not sufficient to unify a work of fiction in which the other elements are incoherent. But style can work in co-operation with the other elements of fiction to produce a final unity. A loosely, though not incoherently, plotted novel like *The Sun Also Rises* benefits especially from the unity of style that reflects the controlling mind and personality of Ernest Hemingway.

THE ELEMENTS OF STYLE: By style we mean the verbal texture of literature, the author's way of using language. In short, we mean everything the author does with words, including his way of arranging words into such larger units as sentences. For purposes of simplification, we shall consider this topic under three headings: diction, imagery, and syntax.

DICTION

By diction is meant simply the author's choice of words. Our purpose in the analysis of diction is to recognize the choices the author has made and to infer when possible the reasons for which the choices have been made. Our assumption is that any choice may be significant and that the sum of choices in a whole work will certainly be so. As we turn our attention from the diction of a brief passage to that of an entire story or novel, we look for the author's guiding principles of selection, for hints of a pattern in the choices he has made. We may undertake the same kind of investigation of the diction in the total body of a writer's work, seeking to discover what kind of choices the writer habitually makes and for what reasons.

DENOTATION AND CONNOTATION: The analysis of diction always leads to some consideration of the denotations and connotations of the words chosen by the author. A word's denotation is simply its dictionary meaning; its connotations are the suggestions and associations aroused by it. A number of different words may have essentially the same denotation, while differing significantly in their connotations. Is a man who reveals the shady activities of his business associates to an investigating agency a "stool pigeon" or "an honest man doing his duty as a citizen?" The difference between the two terms, and it is certainly considerable, is largely a matter of connotation. The first term suggests contempt, the second suggests admiration. Connotations may, of course, be used in far more subtle ways than this.

A first question we may ask in any particular analysis is, to what extent does the writer exploit the suggestive powers of language based on the connotations of words? Some writers, we will discover, choose a diction in which there is a minimum of suggestion or connotation and maximum of statement or denotation. Other writers seem almost to make suggestiveness their only principle of selection. The suggestiveness or lack of it in a given writer's diction will, however, always be relative. A language absolutely without connotation is impossible in fiction, and a language absolutely without denotation is no language at all.

Denotation—An Example from Swift: The diction of *Gulliver's Travels* by Jonathan Swift may seem to take little advantage of the suggestive powers of language. Here, for instance, is a passage describing the Emperor of Lilliput:

> He is taller, by almost the breadth of my nail, than any of his court, which alone is enough to strike an awe into the beholders. His features are strong and masculine, with an Austrian lip and arched nose, his complexion olive, his countenance erect, his body and limbs well proportioned, all his motions graceful, and his deportment majestic.

This is about as close to pure denotation as we can expect a passage of prose fiction to come. The meaning of the passage is little more than the sum total of the dictionary meanings of the words that make it up.

Why should a writer so purify his language of the suggestiveness that other writers strain to achieve? There are a number of reasons for the series of choices Swift makes in this passage.

Some of these reasons have to do with period style, the norm of prose in the first half of the eighteenth century. We shall not here enter into a dissertation upon this subject.

Even to a reader familiar with the period style Swift's diction seems unusually pure of connotations. Let us note as a partial explanation that Swift's plot, involving at this point Gulliver's adventures in a land whose inhabitants are approximately one-twelfth the size of normal human beings, is itself fantastic. Perhaps Swift felt that the greatest sobriety of style was necessary if the audience was to accept the fantasy.

Further, *Gulliver's Travels* employs a first-person narrator. The plainness of the diction may therefore be seen as a reflection of this narrator's character. He is, in spite of his fantastic adventures, not a very imaginative man.

Finally, Swift was deeply suspicious and fearful of the irrational elements in human character, and this attitude is reflected throughout *Gulliver's Travels*. The suggestiveness of language is not based primarily on reason, and the writer who exploits it is therefore appealing to the non-rational side of man's nature. Such an appeal would violate Swift's purpose in his satirical narrative, which is to encourage men to act more reasonably.

The emphasis on denotation in Swift's diction, then, seems based both on the needs of the work and on the qualities of Swift's mind and personality.

Connotation—An Example from Poe: The American Edgar Allan Poe is a very different sort of writer. Here is the first sentence of his famous story "The Fall of the House of Usher."

> During the whole of a dull, dark, and soundless day in the autumn of the year, when the clouds hung oppressively low in the heavens, I had been passing alone, on horseback, through a singularly dreary tract of country, and at length found myself, as the shades of evening drew on, within view of the melancholy House of Usher.

The diction here is characterized by the vagueness of denotation. Just how low is "oppressively low"? What, precisely, does a "dreary tract of country" look like? And how can a house be "melancholy," since the dictionary meaning of the adjective has to do with a human emotional state.

In short, Poe is choosing his words primarily for their connotations, for their suggestive power. His method is, in itself, as legitimate as Swift's and as suited to the demands of his story and his temperament.

A Combination—An Example from Thackeray: Swift and Poe come close to the extremes of statement and suggestion in diction. Few writers go so far in either direction. A diction relying more on connotation than that of Swift and more on denotation than that of Poe is closer to the norm. In the following passage from Thackeray's *Vanity Fair,* connotations reinforce the general drift of denotations. Mr. Osborne and his daughters are about to go to dinner:

> The obedient bell in the lower regions began ringing the announcement of the meal. The tolling over, the head of the family thrust his hands into the great tail-pockets of his great blue coat with brass buttons, and without waiting for a further announcement, strode downstairs alone, scowling over his shoulder at the four females.

Thackeray's control of connotations contributes to our sense of Mr. Osborne's dictatorial nature. He is referred to, not by name or as "father," but as "the head of the family"; the phrase suggests authority. And by speaking of "the four females," rather than "daughters," Thackeray avoids all suggestion of familial warmth and intimacy. And it is, of course, significant that the bell is not merely punctual, but "obedient."

In discussing the passages from Swift and Poe, we concentrated on the significance of denotation and connotation for the work as a whole. The passage from Thackeray exhibits a controlled suggestiveness working within an individual passage to provide insight into character and into the quality of the situation. These selections and our discussion of them should give some indication of the importance of the author's choice of words and of the power that rests in the suggestiveness of words.

IMAGERY

The dividing line between diction and imagery is difficult to draw, for images are made of words and a single word can be an image. Furthermore, the terms "image" and "imagery" themselves, like most widely used critical terms, may take on different meanings in different contexts. In our discussion an image is the evocation through words of a sensory experience; imagery is simply the collection of images in the entire work or in any significant part of the work.

LITERAL IMAGES: Images may be either literal or figurative. A literal image involves no necessary change or extension in the meaning of the words. Swift's reference to the Emperor of Lilliput's "arched nose" is an example of a literal image.

Since fiction deals with people, places, and things, and their relationships in action, it must depend heavily on literal imagery. A basic function of literal imagery is simply to satisfy the reader's demand for specific, concrete detail, his desire to know how things look, sound, smell, taste, and feel. It contributes to the vivid representation of experience that we expect from the best fiction.

RECURRENT IMAGES: While remaining literal in each individual instance, images may make an added contribution to the total design of a story if they recur frequently in the story. In William Faulkner's short story "Dry September" there are a number of images of dryness. For the most part, the individual images are perfectly literal. It has not rained for a long time, and the land is parched and dry. Yet by their frequent recurrence, the images take on a suggestive power, arousing associations with barrenness, sterility, impotence, and frustration, all of which are relevant to the story's meaning.

Recurrent imagery may consist of a number of repetitions of the same image or the frequent occurrence of images that, while not identical, all relate to a single theme. The images may be entirely literal or may be a mixture of the literal and figurative.

FIGURATIVE IMAGES: Figurative images are sometimes called "tropes" or, more commonly, "figures of speech." An image is figurative when it must be understood in some sense other than the literal. Robert Burns's "My love is like a red, red rose" is an example of a figurative image, since the love cannot literally be like a rose.

The line from Burns is an example of a particular kind of figurative image called a simile. A simile is an explicit comparison of dissimilar objects (love and roses), involving the use of such comparative words as "like" or "as." A bolder figure is metaphor in which, because the comparison remains implicit, the statement seems to assert an identification. If Burns had said "My love is a rose," this would have been metaphor.

The frequency with which a writer resorts to figurative imagery is an important quality of style. Jonathan Swift and Ernest Hemingway are two writers, obviously dissimilar in many ways, who are alike in that they make sparing use of figurative imagery. Thomas Wolfe, on the other hand, is an example of a writer of fiction in whose style figurative imagery is a major element. The stylistic austerity of Swift and Hemingway reflects the austerity with which they view human experience. Wolfe's highly figurative style, involving the frequent uniting of dissimilar objects and sensations, suggests his openness to a wide range of experience.

Figurative imagery used recurrently is likely to be significant. In Stephen Crane's novel *The Red Badge of Courage,* men are frequently compared to brute animals. The recurrence of this kind of comparison suggests a skepticism, important to the novel's meaning, about the supposed uniqueness of man's place in the universe. It seems to be implied that man is essentially an animal, driven blindly, like other animals, by his instincts, and not the rational being, acting on the basis of "values" and principles," that he likes to imagine himself.

In the best fiction figurative imagery is not merely ornamental but is an integral part of the total meaning of the work. The rarity of figurative language in Hemingway, like its abundance in Wolfe, is impressive because of its appropriateness to the whole structure of the work. The particular pattern of recurrent imagery in *The Red Badge of Courage* is an important key to that novel's meaning. We may well be pleased by vividness and originality in imagery, but the ultimate question is always, "What does it contribute to the work?"

SYMBOLS: A symbol is basically a kind of image, differing from other images in the use to which it is put. Because symbolism often proves a stumbling block for inexperienced readers, we shall approach the subject of the literary symbol indirectly.

We are all familiar with one kind of symbolism, the kind we call language. For words are symbols of their referents, of the things they refer to. The word "tree" symbolizes a class of material objects.

But as a symbolic system, language is limited. We don't have a name for everything. Even in relatively simple discourse on familiar topics, we must resort frequently to modifiers. Note how many modifiers I have used in the preceding sentence. I had to attach "relatively simple" to "discourse" because we don't have a single name—a symbol—for the thing I had in mind.

But even with the help of modifiers, there are many things that cannot be talked about—as you know, if an experience has ever left you speechless. For we have by no means succeeded in embodying all of human experience in language.

Now a literary symbol is simply the author's attempt to name those many areas of human experience that ordinary language, literal or figurative, is inadequate to deal with. This is all that we mean by the more formal definitions of the symbol we may use occasionally. It is in this attempt that the symbol, while evoking a concrete, objective reality, also suggests an additional "level of meaning" beyond that reality. The writer's use of symbols is continuous with the process of language that we know.

An Example from Melville: Herman Melville's *Moby Dick* is widely regarded as one of the greatest symbolic novels. In reading a work like *Moby Dick* it is important to remember that the white whale does not "stand for" something that can be neatly stated in other words. Rather, Moby Dick names a whole range of experience and perceptions of experience that had never been named before, and for which we still have no name other than the one Melville gave it.

Moby Dick is an instance of a novel essentially symbolic in its design. The symbol may, of course, play a less central role in a given work of fiction. The green light in Fitzgerald's *The Great Gatsby* is an example of a symbol employed to extend the significance of the novel's non-symbolic action.

As this discussion indicates, the symbol, although related to the image, may transcend the limitations of "style" in the limited sense we have been using the term to become the major structural principle of the work. But if we remind ourselves that style is the reflection of the author's way of perceiving and of organizing his perceptions, we can see that even a symbol of the magnitude of Melville's whale remains related to the concept of style.

SYNTAX

To move from the symbolic resonance of the white whale to the frequency of subordinate clauses may seem a crashing anticlimax. Yet syntax, or the way in which the writer constructs his sentences, is as essential an element of style as any we have been discussing.

In analyzing a writer's syntax, we concern ourselves with such matters as the characteristic length of his sentences, the proportion of simple to complex sentences, and so on. These matters are by no means so trivial as they may at first appear. If the sentences of Henry James are characteristically longer and more complicated in structure than those of Ernest Hemingway, this reflects each writer's personal vision of life. For James the perception of experience is a matter of the close observation of fine distinctions; the embodiment of such a vision in prose requires complexity of syntax. To rewrite a story by James in the syntax of Hemingway (or the other way around) would be to change the nature and meaning of the experience.

STYLE AND FIRST-PERSON NARRATION: A special problem in the analysis of style arises in the work of fiction that employs

first-person narration. Is the style with which the reader is con-
fronted properly to be considered that of the author or of the
narrator? Is *The Adventures of Huckleberry Finn* written in
the style of Mark Twain or of Huck Finn? Is *Lolita* written in
the style of Vladimir Nabokov or of Humbert Humbert?

The answer is easy to formulate, if not always so easy to apply.
The style of a work of fiction narrated in the first person may be
thought of as the style of the author so adapted as to reflect the
character of the narrator. Our sense of the degree of adapta-
tion employed in a particular work will, of course, be more or
less sure according to the number of other works by the same
author we are familiar with. The reader who has read most of
the fiction of Mark Twain will have a pretty good notion of
where Mark Twain leaves off and Huckleberry Finn begins.

As a general rule, moreover, we may expect an author to have
more than a little in common with the character he chooses as
narrator. The boxing trainer who narrates Hemingway's story
"Fifty Grand" would never have been used as a narrator by
Henry James, simply because James could never have felt his
way into the mind of a character so different from himself. And
if Huck Finn is younger and more naive than Mark Twain, he
pretty consistently arrives by instinct at the kind of perceptions
that had become Twain's by long experience in observing human nature. We may expect, then, that there will be a consistency between the style of the author and the style of the
narrator he is likely to employ.

TONE

We have, for the most part, been considering style as a self-
contained topic. But earlier in this chapter it was pointed out
that one of the most important functions of style is its contribution to the establishment of tone in the work of fiction.

DEFINING TONE: What, then, do we mean by tone in fiction?
Perhaps the meaning of this term will become clearer if we think
first of a more familiar sense of tone—that is, the sense in
which we speak of tone of voice.

We recognize that in spoken English the same words may add

up to a compliment or an insult. Consider, for instance, the phrase, "Nice work." Say this in one tone of voice, and it's praise; say it in another, and it's an insult.

By tone, then, we mean the expression of attitudes. In spoken language, it is primarily the intonation of the voice (just how one says, "Nice work") that reveals the tone and thereby suggests the attitude. In written language, including the language of fiction, tone is that quality, primarily a quality of style, that reveals the attitudes of the author toward his subject and toward his audience.

An Example from O'Connor: Let us consider, for instance, the subject of the loss of religious faith. For the religious person, or for the person capable, whatever his personal beliefs, of taking religious experience seriously, this is certainly an important subject. With this in mind, examine the following sentence: "My pal Mick Dowling started losing his faith very early, when he wasn't more than eighteen."

The sentence quoted is the first sentence from the story "Anchors" by Frank O'Connor. If we look closely at this sentence, we see that it suggests that the loss of religious faith is a common experience; what is singular about Mick is that he went through this experience rather earlier than most. In short, the subject of the loss of religious faith, which certainly lends itself to an intensely serious treatment, is in this story not treated very seriously at all. Rather, it is treated simply as something, like baldness or matrimony, that happens to most men sooner or later.

The expression in the story of O'Connor's casual attitude toward the loss of faith is a matter of tone. And the tone is in turn dependent on matters of style. "My pal Mick Dowling started losing his faith very early. . . ." The suggestion is clearly that there is a time for losing one's faith; it is bound to come sooner or later, and in Mick's case it comes sooner. The author's attitude toward this potentially shattering experience is one of easy, relaxed tolerance.

But in this sentence the author establishes his attitude, not only toward his subject, but also toward the reader. "Look here," he seems to say. "We're sophisticated adults. We know that religious faith is something one inevitably loses; the only question is when. At any rate, it's nothing to get very excited about."

Not all readers will be able to accept O'Connor's attitude; for some, it will simply be too flippant on a subject they take very seriously. Others will accept O'Connor's attitude easily, because they confuse it with their own attitude (not O'Connor's) of contempt for religious faith. Still others will accept O'Connor's attitude because it is their own. And some will accept O'Connor's attitude, not because it is their own or because they confuse it with their own, but because they see it as an attitude which, however limited, may yet reveal something valuable about the subject.

Whether one accepts or rejects an author's attitude, that attitude is revealed to us primarily in fiction through tone. And tone is dependent on style, that is, on what the author does with language.

UNDERSTATEMENT: In particular, the sentence from O'Connor's story is an example of understatement. That is, O'Connor treats his subject less seriously than most writers would. Understatement has been much favored by modern authors. It seems particularly suited to the contemporary distrust of absolutes. The author who understates does not commit himself very firmly to anything. The particular tact of O'Connor's opening sentence is that it does not take a stand for or against religious faith or the loss of it. Faith and apostasy are presented as elements of human experience, neutral in themselves, but equally available to the writer of fiction.

Understatement may be, as it is in the style of Frank O'Connor, a way of avoiding commitments. (I do not mean this as a condemnation.) On the other hand, the use of understatement may be a way of calling on the reader to react with the full power of his moral imagination. The austere, non-figurative style of Ernest Hemingway is a version of understatement, but its effect is quite different from the understatement of O'Connor. When, in his story "A Way You'll Never Be," Hemingway describes, without the slightest expression of moral outrage, the proper technique of rape, his purpose is certainly not to suggest that rape is a trivial matter. On the contrary, he forces us to see that in a brutal world a deadening of the moral sense is necessary to survival and that this may be the ultimate indictment of the brutality we have come, in our time, to take for granted. Understatement, then, becomes a means of arousing in the reader the complete moral response of which Hemingway's characters are no longer capable.

IRONY: Closely related to understatement, but more clearly focused, is the tone critics usually refer to as "irony." Irony in fiction consists of a discrepancy between what is stated and what is suggested. Irony in its crudest form becomes sarcasm. We say the opposite of what we mean: the words "Nice work," function as a way of saying, "You've really botched it this time."

The writer of fiction occasionally resorts to sarcasm, but, if he is a writer of any distinction, his irony is likely to be more subtle. In *Gulliver's Travels* the King of Brobdingnag, the land of giants, is appalled at Gulliver's boastful description of the weapons of destruction devised by Europeans. "A strange effect of narrow principles and short views" is Gulliver's comment. The reader is expected to see that the true narrow principles and short views are those of Gulliver and his fellow Europeans.

HYPERBOLE: The opposite of understatement is hyperbole, or exaggeration used for rhetorical effect. When, at the beginning of *A Tale of Two Cities,* Dickens refers to the period of the French Revolution as "the best of times" and "the worst of times," he is indulging in hyperbole. The effect of hyperbole in this particular instance and in many others in fiction is a dramatic heightening. We know that no one time can truly be singled out as "best" or "worst," but we recognize that a given period may seem to be one or the other, or both simultaneously, to those living through it.

THE MIDDLE STYLE: Hemingway is given to understatement and Dickens to hyperbole. Most writers fall somewhere in between, exemplifying what we may call the middle style. The aim of the middle style is to present a fair and accurate picture of things as they are. Among modern American novels Fitzgerald's *The Great Gatsby* may be mentioned as a superlative example of the middle style.

Because it avoids extremes, the middle style may seem a kind of ideal. But the avoidance of extremes is not necessarily the highest of literary values. We should sorely miss the work of such "extremists" as Hemingway, Faulkner, Dickens, and Dostoevsky.

SENTIMENTALITY: Failures in tone occur when the attitude of the author seems somehow inadequate to the material presented. Such failures often take the form of sentimentality, the attempt to impose upon the material a greater emotional burden than it can comfortably bear. The death of Little Nell, in Dickens' *The Old Curiosity Shop,* is a classic example of sentimentality. Because Nell is a purely artificial figure, more idealized doll than child, the emotion Dickens tries to stir up by her death is excessive. Bret Harte and O. Henry are two American writers often accused of sentimentality.

Although sentimentality usually involves some exaggeration, it should not be confused with legitimate uses of hyperbole. The line between legitimate and illegitimate exaggeration is, however, not always clear, and intelligent readers may sometimes disagree in their evaluation of particular passages. The question is whether exaggeration is justified by context or by its function in the work as a whole.

INHIBITION: Another kind of failure of tone is inhibition, the author's failure to give due emotional weight to his material. In our time the example of Hemingway has led many lesser writers to an inappropriate use of understatement. In Hemingway's best work, understatement is a form of compression, releasing a powerful emotional impact. In many of Hemingway's imitators, understatement seems merely the admission of emotional sterility. Recognizing again the possibility of honest disagreement, I would mention John Hersey's *A Bell for Adano* and much of the more recent work of John O'Hara as examples of inhibition. James Gould Cozzens' controversial novel of a few years back, *By Love Possessed,* also seems to me to fail on grounds of inhibition. Cozzens, of course, is more in the tradition of James than of Hemingway, but the intricacy and introspection of the Jamesian manner can also degenerate into inhibition.

CONCLUSION: The present chapter has, of necessity, only scratched the surface of the closely related topics of style and tone. Ultimately, only wide experience in reading fiction can turn a reader into a competent judge of style and tone. But to neglect these elements in analysis is to neglect the very sources of vitality in fiction.

CHAPTER 6

STRUCTURE AND TECHNIQUE

INTRODUCTION: There are a number of elements of fiction that, while important in what they can contribute to the total work, are not easily classified under the general headings covered in the earlier chapters of this book. This chapter is concerned with these elements, introduced under the properly vague categories of structure and technique. The same elements might with equal justice have been classified simply as "Miscellaneous."

DESCRIPTION

DEFINING DESCRIPTION: The first of these miscellaneous elements we shall discuss is description. By description we mean the direct presentation of the qualities of a person, place, or thing. For some, description extends to the presentation of non-material qualities, as when the author tells us directly of the moral nature of the character. In this chapter, however, description has a more limited meaning. It covers only the presentation of sensory qualities. The author is engaging in description if he tells us that a character is a tall man, but not if he tells us that a character is a good man. It is, of course, a proper part of description to suggest moral and spiritual qualities as these may seem to be embodied in physical details.

An Example from Dickens: Rather than continue to discuss description at this abstract level, let's look at an example of it. Here is a description of a character from Charles Dickens' *Bleak House*:

> Mr. Chadband is a large yellow man, with a fat smile, and a general appearance of having a good deal of train oil in his system.... . Mr. Chadband moves softly and cumbrously, not unlike a bear who has been taught to walk upright. He is very much embarrassed about the

arms, as if they were inconvenient to him, and he wanted
to grovel; is very much in a perspiration about the head;
and never speaks without first putting up his great hand,
as delivering a token to his hearers that he is going to
edify them.

This is brilliant description on many counts. It is, first of all, a
vivid rendition of the physical presence of Mr. Chadband.
But, more than this, without departing explicitly from description, the passage suggests a good deal about the character of
Mr. Chadband.

How does Dickens achieve his effects? We might note, for one
thing, that there is nothing haphazard about Dickens' choice of
details. He makes no effort to tell us everything about Mr.
Chadband's appearance. Rather, he concentrates on the oiliness
and the awkwardness of the character. The second quality is
suggested in images ("not unlike a bear," "as if . . . he wanted
to grovel") indicating that Chadband barely qualifies as a
human being. And this in turn lends irony to the detail of
Chadband's raising his hand as if about to edify his hearers.

Selection and Arrangement: In this passage of description,
then, we see selection and arrangement at work. Effective description is not merely a matter of the writer's including all the
details he can think of. Rather, the writer must select those
details most appropriate to his purpose and arrange these
details so as to insure that his purpose is fulfilled.

Description is a relatively static element in fiction. In the passage from Dickens, for instance, the story comes to a halt while
Dickens presents Mr. Chadband to us. But notice that Dickens
includes movement ("Mr. Chadband moves softly and cum-
brously . . .") in his description, and that the last detail he
includes, that of the raising of the hand, is well chosen to lead
naturally back into action. Dickens forces us to wait expectantly
for the edifying words of Mr. Chadband.

The description of the Emperor of Lilliput from *Gulliver's
Travels,* quoted in the preceding chapter of this book, is much
less vivid, much more matter-of-fact, than Dickens' description
of Chadband. The flatness of Swift's description is, of course,

not an artistic flaw. Swift is employing a first-person narrator, and this means that passages of description may reveal at least as much about the narrator as about the person, place, or thing described. The very matter-of-factness with which Gulliver describes so remarkable a figure as the Emperor suggests Gulliver's stable and unimaginative personality.

Successful description then, is a matter of selection and arrangement based on the needs of the passage in itself and as part of the whole work. Although specifically concerned with physical details, good description may suggest nonmaterial qualities as well. Although descriptive passages are of their nature relatively static, the better writers of fiction will avoid too sharp a sense of contrast between description and the dynamic development of the narrative.

We have concentrated on the passage devoted primarily or exclusively to description. Often, of course, description is absorbed into the depiction of action. Most of what we have said of the descriptive passage applies with a few modifications to description so absorbed into narrative.

NARRATIVE TECHNIQUE

PANORAMA AND SCENE: We turn now from description to narrative technique, to ways of telling the story. A distinction commonly observed by critics is that between the panoramic and the scenic techniques. While these terms may not be familiar to the general reader, the techniques to which they refer certainly are.

Examples from Hawthorne: Rather than beginning our discussion by trying to define these terms abstractly, let's look again at two passages we discussed in relation to plot in the first chapter. These are the opening passages of Hawthorne's stories, "Young Goodman Brown" and "My Kinsman, Major Molineux." Here again is the passage from "Young Goodman Brown."

> Young Goodman Brown came forth at sunset into the street at Salem village; but put his head back, after crossing the threshold, to exchange a parting kiss with his young

wife. And Faith, as the wife was aptly named, thrust her own pretty head into the street, letting the wind play with the pink ribbons of her cap while she called to Goodman Brown.

This is scenic. It resembles in its manner of presentation a scene from a play or movie. We are close to the particulars of action, in both a spatial and temporal sense. Spatially we are close enough to observe the wind playing with Faith's pink ribbons. Temporally, there is a close relationship between the time it takes us to read of these actions and the time it takes the characters to perform them.

Now let's examine the opening of "My Kinsmen, Major Molineux."

After the kings of Great Britain had assumed the right of appointing the colonial governors, the measures of the latter seldom met with the ready and generous approbation which had been paid to those of their predecessors, under the original charters. The people looked with most jealous scrutiny to the exercise of power which did not emanate from themselves, and they usually rewarded their rulers with slender gratitude for the compliances by which, in softening their instructions from beyond the sea, they had incurred the reprehension of those who gave them. The annuals of Massachusetts Bay will inform us, that of six governors in the space of about forty years from the surrender of the old charter, under James II, two were imprisoned by a popular insurrection; a third, as Hutchinson inclines to believe, was driven from the province by the whizzing of a musket-ball; a fourth, in the opinion of the same historian, was hastened to his grave by continual bickerings with the House of Representatives; and the remaining two, as well as their successors, till the Revolution, were favored with few and brief intervals of peaceful sway.

The contrast between the panoramic technique employed here and the scenic technique of "Young Goodman Brown" should be clear. In "Young Goodman Brown" Hawthorne presents actions that take a few seconds to perform in a passage that takes a few seconds to read. In the passage from "My Kinsman,

Major Molineux," he disposes of forty years (and six governors) in a single sentence. In "Brown" the physical setting is
clearly presented and severely limited: the threshold of the
home of Goodman Brown and his wife, Faith. In "Molineux"
the physical setting is highly generalized: the colonies in general
and the Massachusetts Bay Colony in particular. The actions
in "Brown" are individual; those in "Molineux" are repre-
sentative. The passage from "Brown" has the directness of dramatic presentation; that from "Molineux" has the indirectness
of narrative summary. In the passage from "Brown" we are
hardly aware of the narrator (the phrase "aptly named" is the
only reminder of his presence); in "Molineux" we are inevitably conscious of the narrator as he who selects, compresses,
and summarizes the events of a long period of time into a single
paragraph.

In this series of contrasts, we see the difference between scene
and panorama. The difference is not always so clear-cut. A passage of narrative may be a good deal less generalized than the
one we have been looking at from "My Kinsman, Major
Molineux" and still be essentially panoramic. The essence of
the scenic is its presentation of moment-by-moment action,
often involving dialogue; in "Young Goodman Brown" the
dialogue commences in a second paragraph. As a passage of
narrative moves away from these qualities, it tends toward
panorama.

The choice between the panoramic and scenic technique is
then another of the important choices the writer of fiction must
make. To understand something of what is involved in this
choice, let's consider some of the uses of the two techniques.
We must recognize at the outset that we shall usually find both
techniques employed in a work of fiction, although some stories,
for instance Hemingway's "The Killers," are entirely scenic.
The entirely scenic novel is rare, but *A Portrait of the Artist
as a Young Man* and *Ulysses,* both by James Joyce, are essentially scenic throughout.

BEGINNINGS: As the examples from Hawthorne illustrate,
the writer may begin his story with a passage of either panorama or scene. Each method has its advantages. The scenic
beginning is more likely to catch the reader's attention at once,

because of its concreteness and vividness of presentation. But the panoramic technique often has the advantage of clarity. The panoramic opening of "My Kinsman, Major Molineux," for instance, lets the reader know exactly where he is in time and space and provides a context for the specific actions to follow. Knowledge of the historical picture presented by Hawthorne is essential to an understanding of what happens to Major Molineux.

Hawthorne could, of course, have found other ways to provide the reader with the essential historical information. He could have let much of it come out indirectly through dialogue as the story unfolds. But the method he chose is certainly more economical than any other. Moreover, it allows him to get the necessary exposition out of the way at the beginning and to concentrate thereafter on the story's dramatic content.

A similar beginning, summarizing for instance the history of devil worship in the colonies, would have been a disastrous choice for "Young Goodman Brown." The impact of this story depends to a great extent on our gradually increasing awareness as the story unfolds. It also depends on our close involvement with the characters, particularly with Brown himself, an involvement that would be seriously compromised by the intrusion of the panoramic technique.

But Hawthorne demonstrates the mastery of the panoramic technique in this story as well. The last paragraph of "Young Goodman Brown" is a devastating panorama of Brown's life after that night in the forest. The sudden shift to the panoramic overview at this point in the story powerfully suggests the loss of meaning, variety, and vitality in the existence of Young Goodman Brown.

The power that every reasonably sensitive reader must feel at the denouement of "Young Goodman Brown" suggests the kind of effects a writer can achieve by the intelligent use of both panorama and scene in his fiction. We shall now summarize some of the functions panorama can serve when used in combination with scene.

ECONOMY: The panoramic technique contributes to economy.

It should be obvious that the material presented panoramically at the beginning of "My Kinsman, Major Molineux" could hardly be presented scenically within the confines of a single work of fiction. The material of the last paragraph of "Young Goodman Brown" could perhaps be presented scenically, but this would prevent the story from moving swiftly from climax to denouement. By shifting to panorama, Hawthorne avoids the fault of anticlimax, a severe drop in the reader's attention after the high point of interest has been reached. At any point in the story—beginning, middle, or end—the author may use panorama to present economically what, presented scenically, would require an excessive amount of time and space in view of the story's overall design.

CHANGE OF PACE: Shifts from scene to panorama and back again can have the desirable effect of preventing monotony in the structure of the story. We must recognize, of course, that a writer may be willing to run some risk of monotony for the sake of a higher purpose, or that he may, without departing from the scenic technique, depend on devices other than change of pace (e.g., sheer interest in the events of the story) to prevent monotony. As a general rule, however, monotony is something to be avoided, and the change of pace effected by the shift from scenic to panoramic is one good way of avoiding it.

EMPHASIS AND SUBORDINATION: It is the writer's job, not only to present to us the events of his story, but also to suggest the relative importance to the story of those events. That is, he must emphasize what is of primary importance and subordinate what is of secondary importance. The writer has available to him a number of devices for emphasis and subordination. The traditional development from complication to climax (see Chapter 1) is itself a means of emphasis. But the proper use of scene and panorama can also contribute to proper emphasis and subordination. Material of secondary importance, like the historical background of "My Kinsman, Major Molineux," can be presented panoramically, reserving the scenic technique for moments of crucial importance.

That material is presented panoramically does not always mean, of course, that it is of secondary importance. The last paragraph of "Young Goodman Brown" is as important as any other in the story. But this paragraph, as well as being an example of the panoramic technique, constitutes the denouement of the story. The major structural role it plays, as well as the force of the human material it involves, more than offsets the tendency to subordination otherwise associated with the panoramic technique.

TRANSITION: Finally, panorama may serve a transitional function. While the crucial action in a story may be presented scenically, the author must sometimes take steps to lead the reader smoothly and without confusion from one scene to another. In Anton Chekhov's short story "The Lady with a Pet Dog," the memorable moments are presented scenically. But the story covers a rather long period of time, and its events occur in several different locales. The scenes, then, are widely separated in time and place. Chekhov could, of course, have simply juxtaposed the scenes of his story, but this would have produced a jarring effect, suitable for some purposes, but inappropriate to the demands of this particular story. Chekhov therefore uses panoramic passages as transitions from scene to scene.

The emphasis I have placed on the benefits of combining scene and panorama should not lead the reader to infer that the exclusive use of one technique in a story is necessarily a flaw. I know of no examples of a purely panoramic story, but the purely scenic technique of "The Killers" is entirely appropriate to the peculiar kind of intensity, with its concentration on the present moment, that the story achieves. The scenic quality of *A Portrait of the Artist as a Young Man* promotes the imaginative involvement with character that the novel demands. In short, one must always relate the author's use of scene and panorama to the design of the whole.

DIALOGUE

The last element of fiction to be considered in this chapter is dialogue, by which we mean the presentation in fiction of the actual words of characters speaking to one another. We shall consider both the qualities of dialogue and the functions it serves in fiction.

DIALOGUE AND CONCRETENESS: Like imagery, dialogue is
a means of satisfying the reader's demand for concreteness. In
speaking of imagery, we observed that most readers want to
know how things look, smell, taste, sound, and feel. We want
to know this about the people in fiction as well as about the
places and things. Description can tell us a great deal about
how a character looks. It can also tell us something about
how a character sounds: "He had a high, rasping voice." But
the best way to find out how a character sounds is to listen
to him talk. We were introduced to Dickens' Mr. Chadband
in a paragraph quoted earlier in this chapter; now, let's listen
to him talk.

> "My friends," says Mr. Chadband, "peace be on this
> house! On the master thereof, on the mistress thereof,
> on the young maidens, and on the young men! My friends,
> why do I wish for peace? What is peace? Is it war? No.
> Is it strife? No. Is it lovely and gentle, and beautiful, and
> pleasant, and serene, and joyful? Oh, yes. Therefore, my
> friends, I wish for peace, upon you and upon yours."

The experience of hearing Mr. Chadband, the concreteness of
the impression we receive, could not possibly be equaled by
description, however precise. The demand for concreteness is
satisfied only by Mr. Chadband's actual words.

DIALOGUE AND CHARACTER: In addition to satisfying our
demand for concreteness, Mr. Chadband's speech serves another
function: it tells us a good deal about Mr. Chadband. The
empty rhetoric of his utterance, his apparent inability to wish
someone well and let it go at that, his compulsive and patently
insincere sermonizing, all reflect the moral character of Chadband. Dialogue, then, can be an important means of revealing
character.

The proposition that dialogue reveals character can be turned
around to become, character determines dialogue. For if we
feel we know Chadband better after hearing him, this implies
that we assume some consistency between, on the one hand,
what a man is and, on the other, what he says and how he
says it. A consequence of this is that dialogue is often judged
on the basis of its being "in character." That is, we want to

be convinced that the words put in a character's mouth are words he really would use. Dickens is especially adept, among English prose writers, at creating dialogue so closely related to character that, having once heard a Mr. Chadband speak, we recognize his voice immediately upon hearing it again. The least we may expect is that no character in a story will speak words absolutely inconsistent with his character.

NATURAL DIALOGUE: Along with the demand that dialogue should be in character, one often hears that it should be natural. The demand is a legitimate one, but we must be very sure that we know what we mean by it.

We must remember, first of all, that fiction itself is not natural. Fiction imposes an artificial form on material—human experience—that is naturally formless. The essential artifice of fiction extends as much to dialogue as to anything else. When we demand natural dialogue, then, we must have in mind a naturalness that is somehow not inconsistent with a basic artifice.

We must remember further that dialogue is always part of a larger whole, the story. A demand for naturalness that does not consider the design of the whole may turn out, upon inspection, to be a demand for incoherence.

Let's consider some of the things that will always be artificial about even the most "natural" dialogue in fiction.

DIALOGUE IS SELECTIVE: The distance between fictional dialogue and human speech may be more or less great, depending on the needs of the story and the preferences of the author. But some distance there will always be. At the very least, fictional dialogue involves a process of selection from human speech. Ordinary human conversation, even the conversation of the most highly educated and articulate people, involves much that is rambling, irrelevant, and incoherent. How often do we find ourselves groping for words? How often do we, for all our groping, finally fail to say what we want to say? What would a tape recorder reveal to us about our habits of conversation? We might find that much of the time we sound like this: "It's, uh, you know, uh, uh, well, you know, sort of . . . ."

Characters in fiction, even in what we consider realistic fiction, seldom sound like that. This is because the process of selection mentioned above includes the removal of such irrelevancies, and this removal is obviously a departure from the natural.

Of course, characters in fiction do sometimes grope for words. But when this happens, you may be sure that the groping is at least as important as the words. That is, the author makes the speaker's inability to find the words he wants an indication of his character or emotional state or both. This does not in any way affect what has been said of the selective nature of fictional dialogue.

DIALOGUE AND STYLE: Another note of artifice in fictional dialogue is based on the relation between passages of dialogue and the author's style in general. The author must make his dialogue conform to the characters who speak it, but too great a discrepancy between the style of the dialogue passages and the style of the rest would produce a disconcerting effect. Dialogue, then, must be consistent not only with character, but also with the style of the author.

In practice, this does not usually present much of a problem. The same mind, after all, is behind the style and the characterization. It's true that Mr. Chadband's speech would be inconsistent with Ernest Hemingway's style, but it's also true that a Mr. Chadband isn't likely to turn up in a Hemingway story.

A NEW MEANING OF NATURAL: Does all this mean that naturalness must be rejected as a standard for dialogue? Not necessarily. But we must redefine naturalness.

Natural dialogue is dialogue that is like human speech. Well, what is human speech like? Let's take my speech, for example.

In general, my speech is a reflection of my personality and of the background and experiences that have shaped my personality. I am of Irish ancestry and was born near Boston. In part, my speech exemplifies the accent associated with the so-called Boston Irish. I have been in the Army, stationed in Georgia, and I resided for six years in Michigan. I now live in New York. In my travels, I have been exposed to the dialects of the various regions I have visited; I have, of course, also met people from other parts of the country and from other countries as well.

I am a college graduate and hold the M.A. and Ph.D. also. My major field of specialization was English, and I teach English literature and composition now. This may mean that I have developed a greater sensitivity than most to the rhythms and nuances of language, although I suppose it need not mean any such thing. I am not fluent in languages other than English, but I have studied French, German, Latin, and Homeric Greek.

I suppose I am a product of the lower middle class, although the dividing lines between classes are not always clear to me. Neither of my parents completed high school. I am the third of four children. And one of my brothers is a college graduate. My other brother and my sister are not.

This has been a random listing of some of the things in my life that might have affected my speech in such matters as vocabulary, pronunciation, grammar, syntax, and rhythm. The point is that my speech is obviously related to a number of other things. Any one of my readers could undoubtedly draw up a similar list for himself; no doubt many of my readers' lists would differ in a number of ways from my own.

One thing most of us would have in common, however, is that we are native speakers of American English, and our use of the language will certainly reflect this.

Finally, my speech varies according to circumstances. I don't sound the same when bored as I do when excited.

What all this adds up to is that my speech, human speech, the model for fictional dialogue, is one element in a large and complex pattern. I speak as I do partly because of my personality and experiences, partly because of the world I live in and the time I live in it, and partly because of the situation in which I find myself and to which my speech is a response.

If we demand that fictional dialogue should be natural, then, let's mean this: the relation of dialogue to personality, context (e.g., social position, education), and situation in fiction should parallel the relation of speech to the same elements in life. It should be added that the author's style adds to the context in fiction an element to which nothing in life exactly corresponds.

Putting it another way, dialogue in fiction should be natural to the world the author creates, not necessarily to the world in which the author and reader really live.

Natural Dialogue—An Example from Swift: But let's be specific. Is the following speech from *Gulliver's Travels* natural? The King of Brobdingnag is talking to Gulliver after Gulliver has given him an account of "the state of Europe."

> "As for yourself . . . who have spent the greatest part of your life in travelling, I am well disposed to hope you may hitherto have escaped many vices of your country. But, by what I have gathered from your own relation, and the answers I have with much pains wringed and extorted from you, I cannot but conclude the bulk of your natives to be the most pernicious race of little odious vermin that nature ever suffered to crawl upon the surface of the earth."

Now, I don't know anybody who talks like that. I don't know anyone who's that eloquent, for one thing. But is this a natural way for the King of Brobdingnag to address Gulliver in this situation? To anyone familiar with the whole work, the affirmative answer is inescapable.

FURTHER FUNCTIONS OF DIALOGUE: We may note in conclusion three additional functions of dialogue. For purposes of simplicity, our examples will all be taken from "Young Goodman Brown."

DIALOGUE GIVES INFORMATION: Dialogue is one of the means by which the author conveys information to the reader. In "Young Goodman Brown," Brown insists that New Englanders are people of prayer and good work. The Devil, in answering Brown, provides him and us with information that challenges Brown's assertion.

"I have a very general acquaintance here in New England.
The deacons of many a church have drunk the communion
wine with me; the selectmen of divers towns make me
their chairman; and a majority of the Great and General
Court are firm supporters of my interests. The governor
and I, too— But these are state secrets."

We must remember that information imparted by a character
is never as reliable as information imparted directly in the
author's own voice. We know that what the Devil says is true
because it is confirmed by the incidents of the plot. But a
character may be misinformed or may be deliberately lying.

DIALOGUE REVEALS EMOTIONAL TENSIONS: Dialogue may
reveal not only character but also the particular emotional tensions experienced by the character in a particular situation.
The hesitations of Goodman Brown, the speeches in which he
insists he will go no farther with the Devil, tell us a good deal
about his inner emotional state. "There is my wife Faith," he
says. "It would break her dear little heart; and I'd rather break
my own." The speech indicates Brown's unwillingness, but it
also indicates the weakness of his resolve. Simply by arguing
with the Devil, he is inviting rebuttal, and we are not surprised
that he does not turn back.

DIALOGUE ADVANCES THE PLOT: The conflict that dominates the early portions of "Young Goodman Brown," as
Brown argues with the Devil, is developed primarily through
dialogue. Each new speech advances the plot a step further.
When Brown mentions his wife, we know he is nearing the
end of his argument, and when the Devil expresses concern
for Brown's wife, we sense sinister overtones. The speeches
then are not simply casual conversation to fill a few pages,
but an integral part of the development of the conflict which
is plot.

CHAPTER 7

THEME

INTRODUCTION: Theme-hunting is a favorite activity of critics and teachers of fiction. And, since this is so, it's a common activity of students as well. Indeed, the experience of reading the essays of academic critics and the papers of eager students might lead one to believe that writing a story is simply a way of finding a clever disguise for some abstract idea. And why should a writer so disguise his ideas? Apparently, to give critics and students something to do.

For all that theme-hunting has produced excesses that have led one brilliant young critic to declare herself "against interpretation," theme is something that has traditionally concerned writers and that therefore is a legitimate concern of readers. What we need is an understanding of theme that will make us aware of its function and meaning in literature without encouraging us to the excesses and outright absurdities that have become altogether too common.

The purpose of this chapter is to help in the development of such an understanding. We shall be dealing with three basic questions: What do we mean by theme? How do we determine the theme of a particular story? What is the importance of theme in fiction?

THE MEANING OF THEME

To put the matter simply, theme is the meaning of the story. But any experienced reader of fiction will realize that this is not a very informative definition, and even less experienced readers, upon thinking it over, may begin to wonder in what sense a story can mean anything. Our definition, then, is only a first step towards understanding what theme is.

WHAT THEME IS NOT: We may more closely approach the meaning of theme if we devote some attention to what theme is not. Theme is not the moral of the story, it is not the subject, and although I have defined it as the meaning of the story, it is not what most people have in mind when they speak of "what the story really means."

Theme and the Moral of the Story: One doesn't hear much talk about the moral of the story these days. The phrase is used occasionally, but most of the time in a context that makes clear it's being used ironically. But one does hear so much about theme, that one may wonder if "theme" isn't just a sophisticates' word for moral.

If we examine the way both words have been used, we find that they don't mean quite the same thing. By the moral of the story we usually mean a piece of rather practical moral advice that can be derived from the story. The moral must be rather simple, for it must be pretty readily applicable to the readers' own conduct.

The word theme, as used by most critics, also means something that can be derived from the story, and is in that sense rather like a moral. But a theme can be a good deal more complex than a moral and may in fact have no direct value as advice at all. We may conclude that a moral is one of the simpler kinds of theme, while not all themes are morals.

Theme and Subject: The theme of a story is not identical with the subject of the story—at least, not as we'll use the term "theme" in our discussion. Some critics, it is true, do seem to regard the two terms as synonymous.

In the first chapter we talked about subject. Subject, we observed, is what the work refers to. Thus a possible formulation of Flaubert's *Madame Bovary* would be "the problems of a certain kind of middle-class woman." Some might prefer to have the subject stated more abstractly: "dissatisfaction with reality." Others might prefer a more specific formulation: "the dissatisfaction with reality that develops in a bourgeois French-woman as a response to the limitations of her provincial environment."

Any one of these formulations is the formulation of a subject, not a theme. By a theme we mean some sort of comment on the subject, whether the comment is stated explicitly or remains implicit.

Not What the Story Illustrates: Although I have defined the theme earlier as the meaning of the story, we should not fall into the error of regarding the story as the illustration of some "hidden meaning" which might have been illustrated in any number of other ways. This kind of thinking leads to the belief that the details of which the story is made up, and the precise arrangement of those details, are important only as illustration of something else, i.e., the hidden meaning. Hence, once this meaning is discovered, the story itself may be quickly forgotten. A different statement of essentially the same view is that the precise arrangement of detail is the story's form, while its content is some abstraction that we pull out of all this—with the content, in this sense, regarded as what's really important.

People who approach fiction in this way aren't really interested in fiction at all. What they're really interested in is ideas. The interest in ideas is itself quite legitimate, of course, but when it leads to a distortion of the experience of literature, one may regret the effect even while not condemning the cause.

The notion of fiction as a way of illustrating ideas is often related to a latent or overt contempt for fiction. After all, if it's the ideas that count, why do we need all this tomfoolery of made-up characters in imaginary plots? Perhaps fiction exists for people of inferior intellect who are unable to take their ideas straight. In fact some such notion often lurks behind the contempt otherwise intelligent people sometimes feel for fiction. And if fiction is simply an attractive way of packaging ideas, it's hard to know how to refute this notion.

The other form of contempt for fiction is the practical man's feeling that fiction is a form of escape. According to this view, fiction, being made up, has nothing to do with life as it really is. It's simply a way of escaping harsh realities (for practical men, realities tend to be harsh). The practical man then either contemptuously ignores fiction altogether, or condescends to amuse himself with it during vacations, when he is not in the mood for anything "serious."

Obviously, contempt for fiction is not the attitude of this book, or the attitude this book wants to encourage in the reader. It is the position of this book that fiction is neither a way of illustrating ideas nor an irresponsible escape from reality. Ultimately, the end of fiction is to increase the reader's understanding of reality, but it does not achieve this end simply by illustrating ideas.

WHAT IS THE THEME?: If theme is not the moral, not the subject, not a "hidden meaning" illustrated by the story, what is it? Theme is meaning, but it is not "hidden," and it is not illustrated. Theme is the meaning the story releases; it may be the meaning the story discovers. By theme we mean the necessary implications of the whole story, not a separable part of a story.

Most of us want to make some kind of sense out of our experience. We want to know who we are; we want to know where we stand; we want to know what our relations are to other men and to the universe. Theme is the equivalent in fiction to this normal human impulse.

There are two points to be made about this impulse as it operates in life. One is that making sense of experience requires a full recognition of the complexity of experience. I haven't really made sense of anything if I simply ignore whatever in experience is difficult, unpleasant, or inconvenient. The other point is that there is always something unique about the sense any one of us makes of experience. You and I may both be religious (or irreligious), liberal (or conservative), optimistic (or pessimistic), but I will not be religious, liberal, optimistic (or their opposites or the many shades between) in precisely the way you are, simply because I am not you.

These points apply also to theme in fiction. Theme in fiction is what the author is able to make of the total experience rendered. And although there will be something general in the theme of a work of fiction, there will always be something unique there as well. We may, for the sake of convenience, be prepared to express the theme of a story in general terms, but we must always be aware of how the general statement has been modified, qualified, rendered unique by all the particular details of the story as it unfolds.

WHICH COMES FIRST?:   Which comes first, the theme or the story? Does the author begin with a theme he wants to express in a story, or with a story whose theme he gradually comes to recognize? Any writer of fiction will recognize that this question as presented is phrased in misleadingly simple terms; the process of writing is more complicated than that. But we can perhaps come to some understanding of our subject by pursuing this inquiry a bit further, for all the danger of over-simplification. Oversimplification is harmful only when we are unaware that we're oversimplifying.

Putting it very simply, then, a writer may begin either with a theme or a story. If he begins with story—say, with a fragment of action—part of the process of writing will be his discovery of what this means to him. Why has it suggested itself to him, and why has he been moved to accept the suggestion, to attempt to develop the fragment as a complete story? The answer will reveal itself primarily by what he is moved to do with the fragment that is his starting point, by the form the story takes as it develops. At some point or other, the author may find that he can express his theme in a sentence or two. But this expression, even though it comes directly from the author, will only be a simplification of the complex process of discovery that is the story itself.

Or the writer may begin with theme. He may have some view of human experience he wants to express and will undertake to write a story for the purpose of expressing it. But to express a theme, at least to express it in fiction, is not merely to illustrate it. Fiction involves character and action, and character and action have a way of making their own demands on an author. In giving life to a character, in working out the process of an action, the writer will find himself doing much more than illustrating a theme. He is producing an independent creation with its own existence and its own vitality. If the author refuses to accept this, he will wind up producing a lifeless, unconvincing fiction that is at the same time not likely to be an adequate expression of the initial theme. At least, we may assume that a theme sufficiently important to an author to move him to the hard work of writing a story cannot be adequately expressed in a story that is lifeless and unconvincing.

WRITING IS DISCOVERY: The general truth involved here is that the act of writing is not merely an act of expression; it is also an act of discovery. To illustrate this point, let's consider my experience in writing this book. The subject of this book is one to which, as a student and a teacher, I have given years of thought. Presumably, my job in this book is simply to express the thoughts I have formed over the years. And the book is written to a plan. Before writing the first word of the first chapter, I organized my thoughts into notes and made a detailed outline of what the book was to contain.

Yet this book contains many ideas that I never thought of before. I discovered them in the act of writing. I am gradually finding out what I think about fiction by writing a book about it. Paul Goodman, the brilliant modern writer and social critic, is supposed to have said that when he doesn't know what he thinks about a subject, he writes an article about it. And, according to an old story, a schoolchild once said, "How do I know what I think until I hear what I say?"

Writing is discovery. If this is true of a straightforward job of exposition like the book you're reading, how much more true it must be of the highly concentrated forms of drama, fiction, and poetry!

ALLEGORY: A special case of the relation between theme and the other elements of fiction is the form we know as allegory. Allegory is essentially fiction dominated by theme. Characters and incidents in allegory exist to represent qualities and must be consistent with the qualities they represent. Often, the characters are given the names of the qualities they represent (Patience or Friendship, for example). As a form, allegory does exist to express a theme, and if the story contains anything inconsistent with the theme, this may properly be considered a flaw.

Is there, then, any room for discovery in allegory? The best way to find the answer is to read the greatest of English prose allegories, John Bunyan's *Pilgrim's Progress*. As an allegory, and a great one, this work contains nothing inconsistent with its basic theme. But anyone who has read this wonderful book knows that it cannot be described simply as the illustration of a theme. Much of its power comes from the vividness and concreteness of realistic detail within the allegorical framework. Allegory is not in our time a fashionable form, and most of the allegories of the past are unread today. If *Pilgrim's Progress* still moves us, perhaps it is because of our sense of Bunyan's discovery of the relation between the abstractions that provided him with his framework and the homely, everyday reality in which he lived out his life. *Pilgrim's Progress* is a great allegory and a great work of fiction because it is not simply an illustration of a theme, but a work of discovery and creation.

DISCOVERING THEME

THE SEARCH FOR THEME: Theme, then, is the total meaning discovered by the writer in the process of writing and by the reader in the process of reading. The statement of theme in a sentence or two that one may make while discussing a story can be no more than a useful simplification, a way of pointing to the more complex experience of the story as a whole.

If this is so, then the process of discovering theme must be a complex one. There is no easy way to it. We cannot, for instance, ask the writer what his theme is. If he answers us at all (he probably won't), he can give us, as we have seen, only a simplification of the total meaning of his work. If the theme could be so easily expressed, he wouldn't have had to write the story.

We can discover the theme of a story only by a thorough and responsive reading of the story, involving a constant awareness of the relations among the parts of the story and of the relation of parts to whole. What follows is a discussion of some of the things to which a reader must give his attention in the search for theme.

THEME AND CHARACTER: As a major element in fiction,

character is obviously of major importance for theme. One matter to be kept in mind in reading is the kind of characters the story deals with. If a writer like Henry James seems characteristically drawn to highly sensitive, highly articulate men and women, we may feel justified in assuming that he finds a special value in the lives of such people, that they mean something to him. If a writer like Nelson Algren, on the other hand, populates his fictional world largely with pimps, streetwalkers, drug addicts, sex deviates, and petty thieves, this must indicate that Algren regards the lives of these outcasts as significant. F. Scott Fitzgerald's fascination with the very rich suggests a great deal about the meaning experience has for him.

PLOT AND THEME: Plot is what the characters do and what happens to them. A first question about plot and theme is whether the author's characters do things, or whether things happen to them. The characters of Henry Fielding, on the one hand, do things, while things tend to happen to the characters of Thomas Hardy and Theodore Dreiser. This difference indicates something about the author's view of the extent to which man can control his destiny. We must be prepared, of course, for a highly complex mixture of these two possibilities.

We must also ask what kind of things the characters do and what kind of things happen to them. The characters of Hemingway engage extensively in physical action, in the life of the senses, while the principal actions in the fiction of Henry James tend to be acts of intellect and conscience. Such tendencies suggest something about the author's sense of what kind of actions are most significant and most revealing.

MOTIVATION AND THEME: By motivation we mean the reasons why the characters do what they do. First we must ask whether the actions in the story are clearly motivated. The absence of clear motivation may be an artistic flaw, but we should not arrive too hastily at such a conclusion. The absence of clear motivation in some of Joseph Conrad's fiction is a legitimate reflection of Conrad's sense of the mystery of the human personality.

What kind of motives stir the characters to action? What particular motives seem to dominate them? If all the principal characters in a given story seem motivated by greed, this seems to suggest some evaluation of human character. To what extent does the author engage in the psychological analysis of motives? Sherwood Anderson, in stories like "I Want to Know Why," seems especially concerned with the psychological states underlying our actions and decisions; but psychological analysis is not a major concern of all writers. The motives that interest Fitzgerald in *The Great Gatsby,* for instance, are not primarily psychological. When we are told that Gatsby lives up to his own Platonic conception of himself, we are being given motivation, but not psychological motivation of the kind that concerns Anderson.

To what extent do the characters understand their own motives? Many of the writers often called "naturalists," including Stephen Crane, Frank Norris, Theodore Dreiser, and James T. Farrell, make much of their characters' failure to understand themselves.

SETTING AND THEME: What role does environment play in the lives of the characters? In Thomas Hardy's *The Return of the Native* and in George Eliot's *Middlemarch* the characters seem dominated by environment. A writer's reliance on what we have called a "neutral setting" (see Chapter 3) suggests that for him factors other than environment are of crucial importance in human experience.

What kind of setting does the author prefer? The exotic setting of a story like Conrad's "The Heart of Darkness" is not irrelevant to its total meaning. The urban setting of James T. Farrell's fiction, the rural settings favored by William Faulkner are reflections of the experience, mind, and values of the authors.

POINT OF VIEW AND THEME: The point of view from which the story is told can have great thematic importance. The use of a limited point of view may be related to a distrust of general overviews of experience. Or it may suggest that what we make of information is more important than the information itself. The omniscient point of view may suggest a confidence in our ability to arrive at a full understanding of experience.

STYLE AND THEME: The relation of style to theme was considered in the chapter on style. Style, we have said, is the reflection of the author's way of perceiving experience and of organizing his perceptions. It is, then, a basic element in the total meaning of the story. The reader is referred to Chapter 5 for a further discussion of this point.

TONE AND THEME: The attitudes the author takes toward his material and toward the audience are obviously crucial to theme. And tone is the term we use for the expression of these attitudes in fiction. For Frank O'Connor, the loss of religious faith is a subject to be treated lightly; for Graham Greene the same subject calls for the most serious treatment. This difference in tone is obviously related to a difference in meaning.

VALUES AND THEME: By values we mean our sense of good and bad, of desirable and undesirable. What are the values of the characters in the story and which of these values, if any, does the author seem to endorse? What seems to be the author's sense of the highest end, and what values seem to promote that end?

The search for theme, then, is the search for the force that unifies the many diverse elements that make up the work of fiction.

THEME IN "YOUNG GOODMAN BROWN":   The taciturn President Calvin Coolidge was once asked what had been the subject of the minister's sermon at a church service he had attended. "Sin," he replied. "But what did the minister say about it?" the questioner pursued. "He was against it."

Sin may also be considered the subject of Nathaniel Hawthorne's "Young Goodman Brown," but what he says about it is rather more complex than the theme of the sermon Coolidge heard. The climax of Hawthorne's story occurs when Brown discovers his wife, Faith, among the sinners. This discovery is one of a series. Brown has found that virtually the entire population of Salem village, including its most respected citizens, has come to take part in the diabolical ritual. And the Devil's comments make clear that he has friends and followers throughout New England.

Now, it is certainly not Hawthorne's point that New England is a uniquely wicked place. The Devil talks about New England because Brown does. The Devil might have said he has friends and followers throughout the world. The story seems to suggest, then, that we are all sinners. Now this in itself is a fairly significant statement, especially if seen as a rejection of the Puritan tradition's division of mankind into the elect and the damned. But there is obviously more to the story than this, for if this were the theme we could not account for the denouement of the story.

The denouement reveals that Brown is unable to accept the insight provided by his experience in the forest.

> A stern, a sad, a darkly meditative, a distrustful, if not a desperate man did he become from the night of that fearful dream. On the Sabbath day, when the congregation were singing a holy psalm, he would not listen because an anthem of sin rushed loudly upon his ear and drowned all the blessed strain. When the minister spoke from the pulpit with power and fervid eloquence, and, with his hand on the open Bible, of the sacred truths of our religion and of saint-like lives and triumphant deaths, and of future bliss or misery unutterable, then did Goodman Brown turn pale, dreading lest the roof should thunder down upon the gray blasphemer and his hearers. Often, awaking suddenly at midnight, he shrank from the bosom of Faith; and at morning or at eventide, when the family knelt down at prayer, he scowled and muttered to himself, and gazed sternly at his wife, and turned away. And when he had lived long, and was borne to his grave a hoary corpse, followed by Faith, an aged woman, and children and grandchildren, a goodly procession, besides neighbors not a few, they carved no hopeful verse upon his tombstone, for his dying hour was gloom.

It is clear enough that Hawthorne does not endorse Brown's response to what he has seen, for this response cuts Brown off from his fellow man and condemns him to a life and death of gloom.

The reasons for Brown's response are to be found in his attitude toward Faith. "Well, she's a blessed angel on earth; and after this one night I'll cling to her skirts and follow her to heaven." But Faith is not a blessed angel; she is a human being, capable, like Brown himself, of sin. Brown idealizes his wife. And when he finds her among the sinners, he goes to the other extreme. "Come, devil; for to thee is this world given."

Brown can see his wife only as an angel or as a devil. He cannot see her as a woman. His attitude towards his wife is his attitude towards the world. Brown cannot accept a mixed view of human nature. In the gloom to which this failure leads him we find the key to the story's theme.

We might state that theme like this: "It is essential to develop a realistic view of man, accepting both his capacity for good and his capacity for evil." But, it must be remembered, this is only a simplification of the richly complex experience of the story.

THEME IN FICTION

THE IMPORTANCE OF THEME: It is possible to overestimate the importance of theme in fiction. When this happens, you have the view, discussed earlier, that the work of fiction is simply the illustration of a theme. It is also possible to underestimate its importance. This is what is involved in the view of fiction as meaningless escape. As we have seen, fiction is neither mere illustration, nor is it meaningless. Let's try to establish, as clearly as we can, the precise importance of theme in fiction.

Theme, we have seen, is the reflection in fiction of the human desire to make sense of experience. Since it reflects so basic and universal a desire of mankind, it is an important part of the basic and universal appeal of fiction.

Fiction is in fact one of the ways by which we make sense of experience. Experience itself, as we have said in other connections, is formless. By giving form to experience in fiction the writer clarifies the meaning of experience for himself. The act of constructing a story is itself an act of moral evaluation. If a writer makes an incident the climax of a story, he is asserting by doing so that that incident is important.

The understanding of experience we can hope to derive from fiction is not, of course, identical with that we may derive from philosophy or science. These disciplines are necessarily and properly abstract. But fiction has the concreteness of experience itself. It imposes meaning on experience, not by abstract statement but by form. Fiction, then, offers us a kind of wisdom not to be derived, on the one hand, from experience itself or, on the other hand, from philosophy and science. The theme of fiction is entirely incarnated in the concrete · experience of fiction.

Theme has still further importance in fiction. We have noted at appropriate points in our discussion the contribution to unity of such elements as plot and point of view. But theme is the ultimate unifying element in fiction. It is in response to the pressures of theme that the author shapes plot and brings character into being, and it is theme, whether consciously stated or not, that provides the writer with his most important principle ·of selection.

THE UNACCEPTABLE THEME: If theme is so important in fiction, is it possible for a reader to accept a story whose theme he finds unacceptable? Suppose one does not accept, for instance, the view of human nature implied by "Young Goodman Brown." Must one then condemn the story?

The answer to this question is rather complicated. We can hardly assert that the only good story is the one the reader agrees with. But we don't want to pretend that the unacceptable theme doesn't present any problems whatever.

Let's distinguish first of all between themes that we decide, after thinking it over, are unacceptable and themes that we reject at once as unworthy of our attention. The second kind of theme we'll put aside for the time being. But there seems no reason why we can't admire a story embodying a theme of the first sort. Even the reader who, on whatever grounds, rejects the theme of "Young Goodman Brown" must admit that the story is an honest attempt to make sense out of human experience. One may honor that attempt without accepting the theme.

This still suggests that, other things being more or less equal, the reader may prefer the story whose theme he finds acceptable to the story whose theme he finds unacceptable. And the reader will almost certainly reject the story whose theme he finds unworthy of serious attention.

But since theme does not come to us in a pure state in fiction, it is obviously absurd to judge a story on theme alone. Vitality of characterization, precision of style, and intensity of plotting are among the qualities we may value in a work whose theme we do not accept.

THEME AND VISION: The views I have stated on the problem of evaluating a story whose theme I cannot accept are not precisely my own. I have stated them here, as fairly as I can, because they are commonly held by intelligent and experienced readers. What follows is a statement of my own views on theme and meaning in fiction. I shall preface these remarks by pointing out that my approach tends to reduce the importance of theme in evaluating a story, without at the same time denying the importance of theme in the pattern of fiction.

For me, what is of first importance in fiction is not the theme but the vision, which is simply a word for the author's total response to experience, his total relation to the universe. It is in the nature of the writer's vision that it cannot be reduced to a phrase or a sentence any more than his entire personality can be so reduced, for his vision is precisely his personality as it gets into his fiction.

What good fiction allows me to do is look at human experience through someone else's eyes, the eyes of the author. This is far different from the experience of reading a philosophical essay, for instance, which only permits me to hear what someone else says about human experience. The writer of fiction creates a world that is relevant to the world in which he and I live. In his fiction he gives me a direct vision of that world and therefore of my own world.

The importance of this experience is that, by acquainting me with ways of perceiving other than my own, it increases the ways of perceiving available to me. This in turn increases the possibilities of my coming to some kind of understanding of my world and of myself.

Another way of putting it is to say that fiction enriches the imagination. The importance of this was recognized and expressed by the English poet Shelley. In the passage I quote, Shelley uses the word "poetry" to include all imaginative literature, and therefore fiction.

> Ethical science arranges the elements which poetry has created, and propounds schemes and proposes examples of civil and domestic life: nor is it for want of admirable doctrines that men hate, and despise, and censure, and deceive, and subjugate one another. But poetry acts in another and diviner manner. It awakens and enlarges the mind itself by rendering it the receptacle of a thousand unapprehended combinations of thought. . . . The great instrument of moral good is the imagination; and poetry administers to the effect by acting upon the cause. . . . Poetry strengthens the faculty which is the organ of the moral nature of man, in the same manner as exercise strengthens a limb.

The imagination is the organ of man's moral nature, and this organ is strengthened by the experience of literature. This, and not the communication of doctrines in the form of themes, is the function of literature.

It is, then, by the range or intensity (or both) of the writer's imaginative vision that I judge his work, and this vision pervades every element of the work, down to the tiniest detail of verbal style. What is the role of theme in all of this? The essential one of permitting the author to control, to give order to, his perceptions. The theme, in short, is at the service of the vision. It therefore seems to me relatively unimportant whether I accept or reject the theme in itself.

I don't accept the glorification of crime that I find in the novels of Jean Genet (*The Thief's Journal, Our Lady of the Flowers*). But Genet requires his theme to give order to his vision. And his vision contributes significantly to the development of my moral imagination. Therefore I honor his work and am grateful for it.

THE SHORT STORY AND THE NOVEL

INTRODUCTION: Most of what has been said so far in this book applies equally well to the short story and the novel. Plot, character, point of view, theme are all elements common to both forms. Yet the experience of reading a short story does differ in many ways from that of reading a novel, and some discussion of the peculiarities of the two forms seems in order.

LENGTH: A short story is short and a novel is relatively long. More specifically, the term "short story" is normally applied to works of fiction ranging in length from one thousand to fifteen thousand words. Novels are generally thought of as containing about forty-five thousand words or more. Works of prose fiction of from about fifteen thousand to about forty-five thousand words are commonly called novellas.

Length itself may seem a purely mechanical consideration, but many of the important qualities of the two forms are clearly related to length.

THE SHORT STORY

The short story, for instance, is not merely a truncated novel. Nor is it part of an unwritten novel. It's true that works originally published as short stories later turn up as chapters in novels, but you'll usually find that considerable revision has occurred in the process. The length of a good short story is an essential part of the experience of the story.

Edgar Allan Poe settled the matter of a short story's proper length when he said it should be short enough to be read at one sitting. Poe also said the story should be long enough to produce the desired effect on the reader.

From Poe's rules we can derive another: The effect sought in a short story should be one that can be achieved in a work short enough to be read in one sitting.

INTENSITY: What kind of effect is appropriate to the short story? Without seeking to impose artificial limits, we may observe that the short story seems particularly suited to effects of intensity, and to uses of the elements of fiction that tend to such effects.

PLOT AND INTENSITY: The plot of the short story will often turn on a single incident. Let's consider "My Kinsman, Major Molineux" by Nathaniel Hawthorne. The protagonist of the story is "a young man from the provinces," a type that has always fascinated novelists. The young man wants to make his way in the world, and in this desire we certainly have a subject out of which a novel could be made. In fact, it would be impossible to count the number of novels that have been made out of just that subject.

But Hawthorne's interests lie elsewhere. He presents us with a single night in the life of Robin, his protagonist, more specifically with Robin's search for his kinsman. But this night is a significant one in Robin's life. In fact, it becomes a major turning point for Robin. He had arrived in the town to seek the protection of his kinsman, but at the end of the story he is told, "You may rise in the world without the help of your kinsman, Major Molineux."

The short story is commonly based on a single incident that takes on great significance for the characters. Young Goodman Brown's night in the forest, the arrival of two killers in a small town diner—such incidents are typical of the short story.

CHARACTER AND INTENSITY: Development implies time, and the writer of the short story has little time at his disposal. Therefore, characters seldom develop in the short story. Rather, they are revealed to us. "The Killers" gives us Nick Adams as he is at a certain stage in his development. It does not trace his development beyond this stage.

REVELATION: Revelation of character is only one part of the pattern of revelation common to the short story. Note, for instance, that the two stories by Hawthorne discussed in this book are stories of revelation. So is Poe's "The Fall of the House of Usher," discussed in Chapter 5. And so is "The Killers."

TIME AND INTENSITY: The two Hawthorne stories and "The Killers" share another common element: each deals with actions limited to a single evening. (The last paragraph of "Young Goodman Brown" extends the time element there, but essentially it remains the story of one night in Brown's life.) The writer of the short story is naturally drawn to such limited time periods, although some short stories of course cover rather extended periods.

To summarize, we associate with the short story such qualities as compression, concentration, intensity. These qualities are related to the length of the story and to the structural qualities the length suggests.

THE NOVEL

Where the short story compresses, the novel expands. For the intensity of the short story, the novel substitutes complexity. These assertions may provide a starting point for our discussion of the novel.

TIME AND THE NOVEL: The novel is decidedly not meant to be read at a single sitting. Because of its length, the novel is particularly suited, as the short story is not, to deal with the effect on character of the passage of time. Such works as Tolstoy's *War and Peace* and Thackeray's *Vanity Fair* are particularly notable examples of the novel's power in treating this subject.

DEVELOPMENT: One effect of the passage of time is the development of character. The novel permits us to watch this development. A favorite subject of novelists is the growth of a character from childhood to maturity. Dickens' *David Copperfield* and Joyce's *A Portrait of the Artist as a Young Man* are examples.

SPACE AND THE NOVEL: The length of the novel permits expansiveness in space as well as in time. It is therefore not surprising that man in society has been a favorite subject of novelists. Society has both its spatial and temporal aspects. A society is obviously related to place, but one's role in society changes and develops with time.

UNITY: We may bring this brief discussion to a close by observing that the short story achieves unity by exclusion. The author leaves out all that is not absolutely essential. The novel achieves unity by inclusion. The author puts in as much of life as he can control by his theme.

This brief discussion of the two major forms of prose fiction is not meant to be exhaustive. To exhaust the subject would require an additional book. It is hoped that the reader will find this discussion suggestive.

BIBLIOGRAPHY

It would be impossible to list all the books and essays that have been devoted to the subject of fiction. The following is simply a list of some of the most important and most useful works on the subject.

Aldridge, John W. *Critiques and Essays in Modern Fiction, 1920-1951.* New York, 1952. An anthology of critical essays.

Allen, Walter. *The English Novel: A Short Critical History.* New York, 1954. The best one-volume history, full of insights valuable to the student of fiction.

Booth, Wayne C. *The Rhetoric of Fiction.* Chicago, 1961. The most important recent work.

Casill, R. V. *Writing Fiction.* New York, 1962. Aimed at the potential writer of fiction, but enlightening for readers as well.

Forster, E. M. *Aspects of the Novel.* New York, 1927. One of the classic studies.

Gordon, Caroline. *How to Read a Novel.* New York, 1957.

Lubbock, Percy. *The Craft of Fiction.* New York, 1929. Advances a theory of fiction based on the practice of Henry James.

O'Connor, Frank. *The Mirror in the Roadway.* New York, 1956. A study of the modern novel.

Van Ghent, Dorothy. *The English Novel: Form and Function.* New York, 1953. Analyzes eighteen significant English novels.

Watt, Ian. *The Rise of the Novel.* Berkeley and Los Angeles, 1959. A study of the early development of the novel that casts light on the nature of the form.

INDEX